You've Already Got It!

So Quit Trying to Get It

by
Andrew Wommack

Harrison House
Tulsa, Oklahoma

Unless otherwise indicated, all Scripture quotations are taken from the *King James Version* of the Bible.

22 21 20   17

You've Already Got It!
So Quit Trying to Get It
ISBN 13: 978-1-57794-833-9
ISBN 10: 1-57794-833-5
Copyright © 2006 by Andrew Wommack Ministries, Inc.
P.O. Box 3333
Colorado Springs, CO 80934-3333

Published by Harrison House Publishers
Tulsa, Oklahoma 74145
www.harrisonhouse.com

Table of Contents

Introduction

L ike the dog on the cover, most Christians spend their entire lives chasing something they already have. They're always asking the Lord to do something—to bless, heal, deliver, or prosper them—when in truth, they are seeking what they've already been given. They believe God *can* do anything, but not that He *has* (past tense) done very much.

However, the book of Ephesians was written from an entirely different perspective: Everything has already been accomplished in Christ and given to the born-again believer. It's both already done and already ours!

A victorious Christian isn't seeking victory but rather enforces the victory already won through the death, burial, and resurrection of Jesus Christ. We aren't trying to win a battle. We're coming from a battle that has already been won! Jesus has conquered, and we're enforcing His conquest. (Rom. 8:37.)

As believers, we aren't trying to get something from God; we're fighting to receive the full manifestation of what's already ours in Christ. We aren't trying to get healed; we're fighting because we've already been healed, and the devil is trying to steal it. We aren't begging God to prosper us financially; we're fighting the good fight of faith to see the prosperity that's already been given to us manifest. We aren't asking God to bless us, because He's already commanded His blessing upon us. Through believing we've already got it, talking like we've already got it, and acting like we've already got it—we appropriate what the Lord has provided.

It's Already Done!

Understanding that God has already blessed, healed, and prospered you removes the legalistic performance mentality. You won't struggle under feelings of condemnation and unworthiness anymore, because you'll recognize that everything has already been given. In fact, it was supplied long before you ever came along. And since it's a gift (not based on your performance), your worthiness—or lack thereof—has nothing to do with it!

How can you doubt that God would give you something that you know He's already supplied? You can't! The knowledge that He's already done it eliminates all doubt. No more will you pray, "O God, I know You can, but will You please do it for me?" You'll know that it's already done. The question is: Will you receive?

If you understand and embrace these truths, you'll be ruined for much of what's being called Christianity today. The proclamation that "God *can* heal, bless, deliver, and prosper you" sounds good on the surface but is just a profession of what *can* happen. The Word declares, "God has already healed, blessed, delivered, and prospered you." Can you see the difference?

Enjoy God's Provision

This book contains the truths you need to begin experiencing a much greater manifestation of God's power in your life. Your faith will be quickened, your heart encouraged, and your feet firmly set on His pathway of victory.

Stop chasing your tail, and start enjoying God's abundant provision!

CHAPTER 1

How Desperate Are You?

While ministering once in a church, I noticed how the pastor and his congregation wholeheartedly sang these songs about how "desperate" for God they were. Don't get me wrong. I like those tunes and their overall message. However, I prefer to sing "I'm in love with You" instead of "I'm desperate for You."

Desperate comes from the Latin word meaning "despair." Check out these dictionary definitions:

1. Reckless or violent because of despair, driven to take any risk.

2. Undertaken as a last resort.

3. Nearly hopeless, critical, grave, i.e. a desperate illness.

4. Marked by, arising from, or showing despair; despairing, i.e. the desperate look of hunger.

5. In an unbearable situation because of need or anxiety, i.e. desperate for recognition.

6. Extreme because of fear, danger, or suffering greatly, i.e. in desperate need.

"The synonyms for *despair* are hopelessness, desperation, despondency, depression, discouragement, and dejection. All of these nouns denote emotional states marked by lowness of spirits or loss of hope. Despair and hopelessness stress the utter absence of hope and often imply a sense of powerlessness or resignation. Desperation implies absence of grounds for hope, but adds the idea of fighting back, often blindly or recklessly" (New American Heritage Dictionary).

When you sing, "Lord, I'm desperate for You," what do you mean? Are you saying, "Lord, I'm in love with You and want You more than anything else?" If so, that's fine. But according to the dictionary, you're really saying, "I'm in despair because of this extremely unbearable situation. There are no grounds for hope, but I'm anxiously, recklessly, and violently fighting back anyway." If that's what you mean by being "desperate for the Lord," it's absolutely wrong!

Hungry?

The only reason for a Christian to be desperate is if that person doesn't understand what God has already done. The Lord has already blessed us, healed us, delivered us, and prospered us! He loves us and nothing will ever change that. The only reason to be hopeless, helpless, and in despair is if we don't know who we are and what we have in Christ.

We need a full revelation of what Jesus has done for us! That doesn't mean we won't ever have problems. But in the midst of them, we can say, "Father, You've already supplied this before I ever had the need. I know it's there, so I'm drawing near to You. Thank You for revealing it to me!" Christians should never be hopeless or full of despair.

When you sing, "I'm hungry for God," what do you mean? If you're expressing desire, that's fine: "God, I love You and want You more than anything else!" However, a closer look at the dictionary definition of *hunger* reveals "hurt, pain, agony, depression, and despair that accompanies not having your needs met" (New American Heritage Dictionary).

Many people sing, "God, I'm desperate and hungry for You" and mean "I'm so miserable. Life is terrible, but I'm looking for You. You're my answer, and I believe that out there—somewhere—You're going to do something to meet my needs." That's the complete opposite of the revelation of God's Word!

"What's Wrong With This Picture?"

This church had just sung those songs about how "desperate" and "hungry" they were. "O God, we need a move. Touch us. Please, Lord, do something new!" I stood up to speak and asked, "How many of you are hungry for God? How desperate for Him are you?" They all clapped and cheered loudly.

Continuing, I said, "John 6:35 declares: 'And Jesus said unto them, I am the bread of life: he that cometh to me shall never hunger; and he that believeth on me shall never thirst.'"

I asked them, "What's wrong with this picture? All of you just stood and acknowledged that you're hungry and thirsty. Yet this says that you'll never hunger or thirst again. Jesus told the woman at the well the same thing: 'But whosoever drinketh of the water that I shall give him shall never thirst; but the water that I shall give him shall be in him a well of water springing up into everlasting life'" (John 4:14). They immediately became so quiet you could've heard a pin drop!

Now don't misunderstand what I'm saying. I use the term "getting hungry for God" in the sense that you have a deep yearning for Him. My good friend, Bob Nichols, says, "As long as you can live without more of God, you will" and "As long as you can live without more healing, you will." You could plug a number of different things in there like peace, joy, prosperity, etc. But the point is, you must hunger for—strongly desire and focus on—the things of God in order to experience them.

The Lord doesn't come to those who just passively seek Him. You must pursue Him wholeheartedly.

"For I know the thoughts that I think toward you, saith the LORD, thoughts of peace, and not of evil, to give you an expected end...And ye shall seek me, and find me, when ye shall search for me with all your heart" (Jer. 29:11, 13).

This type of hunger is godly.

But if by "hunger" you mean, "O Lord, I'm just so empty. I have no joy, no peace, no hope. God, where are You? I'm desperate for You." That's not right and that's not faith. Yet this is what's being proclaimed and modeled in the Body of Christ today as being a "normal" experience. It's like a person who's sitting in front of a twelve-course meal. Everything they could ever want is there, but they keep crying "I'm so hungry!" They just want pity or somebody to stick the food in their mouth for them. Personally, I have no sympathy for someone sitting before such a feast and whining about how "desperate" they are. If you're hungry, eat!

Draw From Your Well

God has already given us everything. There's a well of living water on the inside of every born-again believer. It's not the Lord's fault if we're hungry and thirsty. It's not time to ask Him to come and touch us. It's time for us to start taking, eating, and drinking of what He's already given!

I'm not saying there's no place for a Christian to ever have problems or discouragement, or that we should always be perfect and just deny reality. Believers do experience hunger in the sense that they feel empty and God seems like a million miles away. But when you experience that, it's wrong to approach Him saying, "O Lord, I just don't feel Your love. Please love me. Do something to show me You care!" You might as well have said, "God, You haven't done anything," because you're blaming Him for your feelings of emptiness and hunger.

Through the revelation contained in this book, I've learned that God loves me infinitely more than I can ever comprehend or need. He can't love me more or give me any more love than what I already have. Knowing this has kept me out of depression and discouragement for over thirty-five years!

There were times when such feelings tempted me. I've had issues and terrible things happen, just like anybody else. I've even had thoughts like, *Man, just get in your pickup and drive. Don't ever come back! I can't stand it anymore. Just walk away!* Although I've had these thoughts, I don't give in to them, because I also have this revelation that God loves me and has already provided everything I need.

So instead of giving in to hunger, discouragement, and despair, I remind myself of God's Word. I don't ever say, "Lord, that's the way it is. Now You must do something brand new to touch me. I'm looking for something else from You." That would be an insult against what He's already done. Instead, I pray, "Father, this is absolutely wrong. John 6:35 says that I should never hunger or thirst again. I know that on the inside of me there is so much love, joy, and peace—all the fruit of the Spirit. (Gal. 5:22, 23.) Everything I need is already there. So, Father, I know that You have done Your part. It's not Your fault if I'm tempted with depression, discouragement, giving up, and quitting. It's my fault. I'm not focused on You. I've let my eyes be taken off of You and put on the problems of this world." I'll just separate myself and spend a day or so fasting, praying, and seeking God. What I'm doing is mining what the Lord has already placed within me. Instead of asking Him to give me something new, I draw out the life that He's already given.

That's why I can truthfully tell you that I haven't been depressed in over thirty-five years. I've been tempted with depression. I've had feelings of depression start to hit me. But within ten or fifteen minutes, I just decide that I don't like depression and refuse to have it. God has given me such joy inside that I can choose to rejoice at all times. (Phil. 4:4.)

Not Passive!

The Word says, "I will bless the LORD at all times: his praise shall continually be in my mouth" (Ps. 34:1).

This isn't telling you to just "fake it 'til you make it." Rather, this is talking about drawing out what's inside of you.

As I've drawn on the joy that God has already placed within my born-again spirit, I've lived a consistently victorious life. In the midst of great adversity, I've experienced continual joy and peace. It's not because I'm never tempted with the other but because I know in my heart that God has already done His part.

I haven't become passive and said, "God, I'm waiting on You." Many people do that and languish while waiting for an epiphany. They sing, "I'm so desperate and hungry! O God, where are You? I'm just a poor wayfaring pilgrim, and it's so miserable down here." Instead, I pray, "Father, I know this isn't right. This isn't what You've done. Your Word shows me that You've already blessed me. I praise You for what You've done!" I start focusing on the Lord and His Word and draw out His abundant life from within me.

That's why I haven't had discouragement or depression last more than a very short time for over thirty-five years now. I simply refuse to yield to them or let them have their effect in my life. That's awesome!

Many people desire these same results, but they think the way to achieve them is to passively ask God to do something and then sit back and wait. If things don't change, and victory—healing, prosperity, blessings, deliverance—doesn't instantly come, they get upset with the Lord, asking, "God, why aren't You doing anything?" That's not it at all.

The Lord has already done everything. However, if you're not seeing it manifest, it's not God who hasn't given—but you who haven't received! Come with me as I take you on a journey that will teach you how to receive what God has already done for you.

CHAPTER 2

Check Your Receiver

Ephesians was written from the perspective of what has already taken place. Paul's opening comments in this letter were:

*Paul, an apostle of Jesus Christ by the will of God, to the saints which are at Ephesus, and to the faithful in Christ Jesus: Grace be to you, and peace, from God our Father, and from the Lord Jesus Christ. Blessed be the God and Father of our Lord Jesus Christ, who **hath** blessed us with all spiritual blessings in heavenly places in Christ.*

Ephesians 1:1-3, emphasis mine

Notice the terminology here: "Blessed be God who has—past tense, it's already been done—blessed us with all spiritual blessings."

Some people argue, "Well, this means only in spiritual things, in an ethereal realm, not in practical, personal ways. It's just in heavenly places that we've been blessed." Really, "all spiritual blessings in heavenly places in Christ" is just an Old English way of expressing the truth that God has already blessed us with everything—and it's in the spiritual realm.

Everything that God has done for you has already been deposited into your born-again spirit. Although it's already there, you must draw it out of the spirit and into the physical realm.

If God has already blessed you, which Ephesians 1:3 clearly reveals, then why do you keep asking Him to bless you? "Come on, Andrew! That's just semantics." No, it's a problem. The reason you keep praying, asking, and seeking God's blessing is because you don't truly believe you're already blessed!

Silence

While ministering to an audience, I often walk over and give my Bible to someone on the front row. Then I ask the people, "What do you think I'd do if that person who already has my Bible came up to me and asked, 'Can I have your Bible, please?'" How would you respond if someone asked you for something you knew you'd already given them? Personally, I wouldn't know how to answer. I'd probably just look at them and think, *You've already got it—so what are you asking for? What am I supposed to do that I haven't already done?*

If you asked someone for something they knew you already had, how would they respond to you? There'd probably be an awkward silence. Sounds a lot like how God often responds to us!

You pray, "O God, please heal my body!" but don't hear a thing, so you wonder, *Lord, what's going on? Why haven't You answered my prayer?* God's probably in heaven scratching His head and thinking, *Now wait a minute. Doesn't 1 Peter 2:24 say that by My stripes you were (past tense) healed? It's already done! I've already placed the same power that raised Christ from the dead inside you. (Eph. 1:19-21.)* If God could be confused, I believe He would be, saying, "I know I already gave this to them, but here they are asking Me for it." That's not the way to approach God!

We pray other stupid prayers too, like, "God, we ask You to come and be with us in our church service today. O Lord, meet with us!" The Word plainly says, "I will never leave thee, nor forsake thee" (Heb. 13:5), and "Where two or three are gathered together in my name, there am I in the midst of them" (Matt. 18:20). God's always with us, but still we pray, "O Lord, come and be with us" and "Lord, go with us as we leave this place." How is God going to answer prayers like that? Do you know what we're doing? We're letting our senses dominate us. Since we don't see Him or feel anything, and nobody's jumped a pew yet, we ask God to come when the Word says He's already there.

Begin To Receive

An appropriate way to pray is, "Father, Your Word promises that You'll never leave us nor forsake us, and when two or three gather together in Your name, there is a special presence of the Holy Spirit. Father, we thank You that You're here. We believe it and we want it manifest. We don't want You to just be here in the spirit realm. We desire to yield to You to the point that You can manifest Yourself in healings, deliverance, joy, peace, salvation, and Holy Spirit baptism. We want You to be free to manifest Yourself and do what You want to do." That's a proper way to pray because you're praying in agreement with God's Word. You're saying, "We believe

Your promises, but we want them manifest. We desire for You to come from the spirit world into physical manifestation!"

Praying, "O God, come and be with us" is incorrect. It means you don't believe that God is there until you can see or feel Him. Then, when someone starts shouting, "I feel the Holy Ghost," you say, "God's here now!" It wasn't that He just showed up. He was there the whole time. You just began to receive.

Wherever you are right now, there are television signals all around you. It doesn't matter if you're at home, in a car, at work, on a bus, or sitting under a tree somewhere, television signals are there. Just because you can't perceive them with your five natural senses doesn't mean they're not present. Even in the physical realm, an unbeliever—someone with zero faith—can prove that there are television signals surrounding you. All they have to do is take a television set, plug it in, turn it on, and tune it in!

When you first see the signal on the screen is not when the station started broadcasting. The signals were there before the television set was turned on. When you turned on and tuned in your set is when you started receiving, but it's not when the station began broadcasting.

What would you do if your television set went blank all of a sudden? Would you call the station and ask them to start broadcasting again? No! You'd check your receiver by turning it to another station. If other channels were still coming in, but that one wasn't, then you might think it's the station not broadcasting. Maybe they're having a problem with their transmitter. But if your television went totally blank, and no channels came in, you wouldn't call the station. You'd know, *My receiver's the problem!* Since 99 percent of the time the issue is with your receiver—not the station's transmitter—the first thing to do is check your receiver.

Pray in Faith

God's the One with the transmitter. He's the Giver of all earthly and spiritual blessings (Eph. 1:3), and He's already transmitted them to you. Everything comes from God, but He's already transmitted. If you aren't seeing them manifest in your life, the problem isn't with God's transmitter. You need to fix your receiver!

Yet, when most Christians don't feel joy, they go to the Lord and ask, "O God, where's my joy? What's wrong? Restore unto me the joy of my salvation!" Have you sung that song? It's a great tune, but the words are actually taken from an Old Testament scripture.

"Create in me a clean heart, O God; and renew a right spirit within me. Cast me not away from thy presence; and take not thy holy spirit from me. Restore unto me the joy of thy salvation; and uphold me with thy free spirit" (Ps. 51:10-12).

David prayed this in repentance of his sin with Bathsheba.

However, for a New Testament believer to say, "O God, cast me not away from Your presence. Please, don't leave me!" is an insult against what Jesus came to do. David didn't have a covenant that promised God would stick with him through anything. The Old Covenant was based upon performance, so God did come and go. Old Testament people weren't born again. They didn't have an eternal redemption the way it's spoken of in the New Covenant. (Heb. 9:12, 14.) However, Jesus promised, "I will never leave thee, nor forsake thee" (Heb. 13:5), and "Lo, I am with you alway, even unto the end of the world" (Matt. 28:20). If you've been born again and don't feel the presence of God, for you to pray this prayer that David prayed and say, "Cast me not away from Your presence, renew a right spirit within me, and take not Your Holy Spirit from me," means that you don't understand what benefits you have in your covenant. You're in unbelief—not believing the New Covenant!

Instead of praying in unbelief and then wondering why you aren't seeing better results, you need to pray in faith! It's the prayer of faith that will save the sick. (James 5:15.) It's the prayer of faith that will bring you deliverance and joy.

Say, "Father, I don't feel like You're here. There's simply no tangible indication of Your presence in my life right now. Everything's gone south. But Father, Your Word says that You'll never leave me nor forsake me, so I know that You're here. Whatever is causing these problems in my life is not You. I know that You haven't forsaken me. I ask You now to help me see what I've done to turn away from You. As I seek You, please help me make the connection and release this life You've placed inside me. I know Your Holy Spirit's still here. I know Your blessings are still here. I'm believing that they'll be released. I refuse to have these other things." That's praying a prayer of faith!

Defend Your Position

There's still a fight. But the fight is to stand in the victory that God has already purchased for you—not to go out and win one. There's a big difference!

While in the army, I discovered that defending a position that was already held is much easier than trying to take a new one. If you were on top of a hill and had the advantage of a defensive position, you could hold it with five men. But a hundred men would be required to take that same position. Much more effort is needed to go conquer something you don't yet have than to defend something that's already yours.

You need to believe that you're already blessed. (Eph. 1:3.) God has already given you healing, wisdom, revelation, prosperity, joy, peace—everything that you'll ever need!

My teaching *Spirit, Soul & Body* goes into much more depth on this very truth. It reveals from God's Word how your born-again spirit is already as perfect, complete, and full of God's blessing and power as it ever will be throughout all eternity.

One-third of your salvation is over. Your spirit is completely saved. It's identical to Jesus. It has His joy, His peace, His knowledge, His love, and His fruit. Everything that's true of Jesus is true of your born-again spirit. There's no inadequacy. It's not in the process of growing up into these things. It's not that these things are in your spirit in seed form, but they have to mature; no, they are already complete and full-grown in the spirit. All you have to do is renew your mind and let these things manifest themselves through you. If this isn't a revelation to you, you need it to fully understand what I'm sharing.

God has already done it. This isn't just "in principle." It's not just written on a piece of paper somewhere. There was an actual transformation that took place in your spirit the very moment you were born again. Now you have love, joy, peace, longsuffering, gentleness, goodness, faith, meekness, and temperance. (Gal. 5:22, 23.) You are—right now in your spirit—identical to Jesus. (1 John 4:17; 1 Cor. 6:17.) The same power that raised Christ from the dead now lives inside of you. (Eph. 1:19, 20.) It's infinitely easier to release something you know and believe you already have than it is to try and go get something you don't.

If you're not absolutely convinced that you've already got it, you'll either submit to or have to battle thoughts that you won't get it. However, once you know it's yours, how could you doubt you'd get it? This is simple, but so profound!

Drawing the Line

When my wife and I first started out in ministry, we were so poor we couldn't even pay attention! The Lord had already blessed us with financial prosperity, but I wasn't cooperating with His laws for releasing it. In fact, I was violating a number of instructions in God's Word. Therefore, we really struggled until I learned some things and adjusted accordingly. God loved us, and we didn't starve to death, but we didn't prosper until we understood how His kingdom works and began to cooperate.

During that period of time, I didn't even have a complete Bible. Mine had gone through Vietnam with me. It was so beat up and marked up that most passages could hardly be read. Also, entire books had fallen out and been lost. Here I was pastoring this little church in Segoville, Texas, without a full Bible!

Right or wrong, I made a decision. "Father, I have to start seeing Your power manifest somewhere. If I can't believe You for enough money to buy a new Bible, how am I going to believe You for enough money to lead people into salvation and see them healed, delivered, and baptized in the Holy Spirit?" I just made an issue out of it, saying, "God, this faith either works, or I'm going to die right here. The outcome of this battle determines whether or not I'm going on." To me, this was non-negotiable.

So I started believing God for a new Bible. All told, it took me six months to get enough money to buy it! It's not that this wasn't my priority. It's just that finances for us were tight. My wife and I would go two or three weeks without food—even when she was eight months pregnant—because we just didn't have it. I'm not exaggerating when I say that it took me six months to believe for the extra twenty-five dollars to go buy a Bible.

To some people, financial "trouble" is having $1,000 in the bank and $1,100 worth of bills. We didn't even have a bank account—much less any money to put in it! There were days when we'd go without a penny in our pockets. I'd even pick up Coke bottles just to get gas money.

Dealing With Doubt

Satan plagued me that entire time. I fought doubt constantly. There probably wasn't a ten-minute period of time during my waking hours for six months that I didn't have some thought like, *It's not going to work. You'll never get it. You don't even have a Bible. Some man of God you are!* I'd have to throw down those thoughts and say, "No! In the name of Jesus, I do have my Bible!" I fought these constant, unrelenting thoughts for six whole months.

Finally, I had enough money. So I went to a bookstore, bought a Bible, and had my name engraved on it. It was mine! After I walked out the door with that new Bible under my arm, I never again doubted that I'd get it.

"Well, of course! Why would you doubt that you'd get something you've already got?" My point exactly!

Do you know why you have to counter this thought, *I'm going to die,* immediately after praying, "O Lord, please heal me"? It's because you don't believe you've already been healed. You believe God can heal you, but you're waiting on Him to do so. That's wrong! God has already released His healing power. You aren't waiting on God to heal you; God is waiting on you to appropriate what He's already done.

Believe and Receive!

It's like that television signal. The signal is already being broadcast. If you aren't seeing the picture, it's not God who isn't transmitting; it's your receiver that isn't working right. You need to get into the owner's manual—God's Word—and start studying. Find out how to turn that thing on, tune it in, eliminate the static, and deal with things to get the best reception.

Don't say, "I'm waiting on God!" That's not how it works. "By whose stripes ye *were* healed" (1 Peter 2:24, emphasis mine). God is waiting on you to believe and receive!

Since I've begun teaching this, I've seen a tremendous increase in the amount of people receiving their healing. They are no longer just asking and waiting on God to do it. Instead, they're believing what the Lord has already done. They're taking their authority and commanding what's already been provided to come into manifestation. The results have been awesome!

My oldest son, Joshua, became sick and looked like he was going to die. Jamie and I fought it, stood against it, and finally he got better. This happened several years in a row. Finally, I saw this coming back on him again and sought the Lord about it. I prayed, "Lord, what's wrong?" He answered, "The problem is that you are fighting to get healed instead of fighting because you've been healed. You're trying to obtain healing instead of defending the healing you already have." Once I understood this, things turned around.

Don't fight to *get* healed; fight because you've *been* healed! Don't fight in an attempt to obtain healing; fight to defend the healing that's already been provided for you in Christ!

Allow this revelation to sink in and change your attitude toward everything you receive from the Lord!

CHAPTER 3

Accepted and Enlightened

"According as he hath [past tense] chosen us in him before the foundation of the world" (Eph. 1:4, brackets mine).

When you cried out to the Lord for salvation is not when He first set His desire upon you. God didn't hear you and all of a sudden say, "Okay! I think I'll respond and send My Son." No, He already chose you. The provision had already been made. Atonement was already an accomplished work. Salvation was just waiting for you to reach out in faith and appropriate it. Although you had to choose to believe and receive, God had already made the provision before you ever had the need, before you were even born, and before you had ever sinned!

> That we should be holy and without blame before him in love: Having predestinated us unto the adoption of children by Jesus Christ to himself, according to the good pleasure of his will, To the praise of the glory of his grace, wherein **he hath** [past tense] **made us accepted in the beloved.**
>
> Ephesians 1:4-6, emphasis mine

Most Christians are trying to do things (live holy, read the Word, tithe, fast, etc.) to make themselves acceptable to God. That's like a person with a stick tied to their back and a carrot dangling out in front of them. They're on a treadmill going nowhere. Every time they reach out and strain toward their goal—it moves! Religion has these Christians constantly looking forward to a time when they'll be accepted by God. They're blinded to the truth that He's already made them "accepted in the beloved" (Eph. 1:6).

The Greek word translated here "accepted in the beloved" is the exact same word rendered "highly favoured" in Luke 1:28. "And the angel [Gabriel] came in unto her, and said, 'Hail, thou that art highly favoured, the Lord is with thee [Mary]: blessed art thou among women" (brackets mine). These are the only two times this word is used in the New Testament. Therefore, being "accepted in the beloved" means you are "highly favoured" of God!

An Accomplished Fact

Most Christians don't believe the Lord's acceptance, favor, and love toward them is an accomplished fact. It's something they long for and hope to obtain, but don't understand that they already have it. The truth is, God loves you—and He can't love you any more than He already does! There's absolutely nothing you can do to make Him love you more—or less.

Now, that's contrary to most religious teaching today. Religion says, "God loves you proportional to your performance." That's not true. You're accepted because of what Jesus did. Ephesians 1:6 declares that you are "accepted *in the beloved*" (emphasis mine). Who's that? Jesus! "In whom we have redemption through his

blood, the forgiveness of sins, according to the riches of his grace"
(Eph. 1:7).

You have already been forgiven—completely! Jesus didn't only
deal with your past sins, which you've confessed. At the cross, He
paid for all of your past, present, and even future tense sin. This is
the "eternal redemption" that Hebrews 9:12 reveals. (My message
entitled "Eternal Redemption" deals with Hebrews 9 in depth. It's
the second part of *Spirit, Soul & Body*.)

If you were asked to write a prayer that believers two thousand
years from now would be able to read and benefit from, what
would you pray? Based on my experience with thousands of
people, the average Christian today would say, "O God, I ask You
to pour out Your Spirit on that generation. Send revival and move
in a mighty way! O Lord, do a new thing on the earth in that day!"
Basically, their whole prayer would be, "God, do something!"

Paul prayed just the opposite!

*That the God of our Lord Jesus Christ, the Father of glory, may give
unto you the spirit of wisdom and revelation in the knowledge of
him: The eyes of your understanding being enlightened; that ye may
know what is the hope of his calling, and what the riches of the glory
of his inheritance in the saints, And what is the exceeding greatness
of his power to us-ward who believe, according to the working of his
mighty power.*

Ephesians 1:17-19

There's a huge difference between what we pray: "O God, go
and touch this person" and what Paul prayed: "Lord, please help
them to see and understand what You've already done."

When you know what God has already done, you'll pray with confidence.

Who's Responding to Whom?

Jesus loves the people you're interceding for much more than you do. It's not your prayer that's making Him love them and move in their lives. He loves them millions of times more than you possibly could! You can't even approach the love God has for the people you're interceding for, but how many times have you prayed for someone and felt, *Lord, if You love this person half as much as I do, You'd touch their life!*

I prayed that way thirty years ago. While interceding for our city, I literally wept, wailed, begged, and pleaded, thinking God had to do something to send revival. I worked myself up into such a frenzy that I pounded the wall and cried out, "God, if You love the people of Arlington, Texas, half as much as I do, there'd be revival!" However, as soon as that came out of my mouth, I knew something was terribly wrong with my theology.

I thought God was responding to my prayer. I believed my intercession motivated and moved Him to do something. I pictured the Lord in heaven with His arms folded, upset with us over how ungodly we were. It seemed to me that He had withdrawn His Spirit and His blessings, and we had to plead with Him to turn His heart back toward us. Many people believe this is the way to pray for revival, but it's absolutely wrong.

Don't misunderstand me—I'm for revival and all of its benefits. I just disagree on how we get there.

Dip In, Draw Out, and Release!

Revival doesn't come by begging the Lord to pour out His Spirit. Neither does it come by pleading with Him to move and do a new thing. Revival comes by starting to believe what God has already done and beginning to walk in His dynamic, supernatural life.

You raise someone from the dead. You open up some blind eyes. You start ministering to people and seeing them set free—and you'll have all the revival you can handle!

Jesus didn't come asking God to pour out His Spirit. After being filled with the Holy Ghost, He simply dipped in, drew out, released, and gave of the Spirit to people. Everything we'd call "revival" happened in Christ's ministry, but not through begging and pleading with God to do something. Jesus simply did what His Father had told Him to do!

Yes, we need revival in our land. But how does it come? By recruiting another million Christians to pray, agree, and fast one day a week asking God for it? No! Revival comes when we seek the Lord wholeheartedly and begin to believe, draw out, and flow in what He's already done. If you catch on fire for God, people will come and watch you burn!

See and Understand

Paul didn't pray for God to do something new. Instead, he said, "Wherefore I also, after I heard of your faith in the Lord Jesus, and love unto all the saints, Cease not to give thanks for you, making mention of you in my prayers; That the God of our Lord

Jesus Christ, the Father of glory, may give unto you…" (Eph. 1:15-17). What? A new thing? Another outpouring? A brand-new wave? No! "The spirit of wisdom and revelation in the knowledge of him" (v. 17).

Paul wasn't asking for something new but that the revelation of what God has already done and is now resident within us would begin to come out!

"Wherein he hath [already] abounded toward us in all wisdom and prudence; having made known unto us the mystery of his will" (Eph. 1:8, 9, brackets mine).

In other words, this wisdom and revelation Paul was praying for has already been given to every believer. It's just that not every Christian is receiving it—they don't have their set plugged in, turned on, and tuned in to it.

He prayed that "the eyes of your understanding being enlightened; that ye may know what is the hope of his calling, and what the riches of the glory of his inheritance in the saints" (Eph. 1:18). You don't need God to do something new. What you need is to see and understand what He's already done!

As a born-again believer, you are now more than a conqueror through Christ. (Rom. 8:37.) You have already been transformed from sinful, unrighteous, and unholy to righteous and holy in Him. (2 Cor. 5:17, 21; Eph. 4:24.) You were delivered out of the kingdom of darkness and translated into the kingdom of God's own dear Son. (Col. 1:13.) The same power (Eph. 1:19, 20), life (Gal. 2:20), wisdom (1 Cor. 1:30), victory (1 Cor. 15:57), anointing (1 John 2:20), and faith (Gal. 2:20) that Jesus had now resides in you. You don't need more of anything!

You just need a revelation of what you already have! That's what Paul was praying: That the eyes of your understanding would be enlightened; that you would know what is the hope of His calling; that you would have a full revelation of your potential in Christ; that you would see what the riches of the glory of His inheritance are in you—a saint!

Focus Your Attention!

Most people imagine the glory of God as being far off. They picture the splendor of heaven—gates of pearl, streets of gold, mansions, etc. But Ephesians 1:18 reveals that the riches of the glory of God's inheritance is in the saints. What's in heaven pales in comparison to what's already inside of you!

You're probably thinking, *That can't be right!* Why? You look in a mirror and see zits, gray hairs, bulges, etc. You survey your emotional realm and notice that you don't feel peace or joy. So you conclude, "This can't be where God's glory is. Surely, it's not here!" God's glory is in your born-again spirit, not your body or soul!

Your five natural senses cannot perceive your spirit. Neither can you "feel" it with your soul (your personality—mind, will, emotions, and conscience). You must see who you are and what you have in the spirit realm through God's Word and then believe it by faith. Most Christians don't know this, but God's glory is already inside their spirit.

If you had a revelation of this, depression would have no power over you! How could you stay down in the dumps when you truly know the hope of your calling and what are the riches of the glory of His inheritance in you right now? In order to stay depressed, you'd have to shut that revelation off and look only in the physical realm at your circumstances and other negative things. But if you focus your attention on who you are and what you have in Christ, recognizing that it's a done deal and that the glory you'll experience throughout all eternity is already inside you, depression would leave, and you'd start enjoying victory. That'll put a shout in a fence post!

CHAPTER 4

His Power in You

Paul prayed that you'd understand:

> ...what is the exceeding greatness of his power to us-ward who believe, according to the working of his mighty power, Which he wrought in Christ, when he raised him from the dead, and set him at his own right hand in the heavenly places, Far above all principality, and power, and might, and dominion, and every name that is named, not only in this world, but also in that which is to come: And hath put all things under his feet, and gave him to be the head over all things to the church, Which is his body, the fulness of him that filleth all in all.
>
> Ephesians 1:19-23

God wants you to see the exceeding greatness of His power toward us who believe. It's the very same power He used to raise Jesus Christ from the dead!

Have you ever prayed and asked the Lord for more power? Where do you think He'd get it? Ephesians 1:19-20 declares that you already have within you the same power that raised Jesus Christ from the dead. That's the greatest manifestation of God's power ever!

Raising Jesus from the dead required more power than creating the universe, parting the Red Sea, or anything else God has ever done. If you could put God's power on some kind of meter that would show how much power is released, I guarantee the power indicators would have all pegged out over the max when Christ arose from the dead. Why? Satan and all his demons did everything they possibly could to prevent the resurrection—but failed!

Ruined!

The large church I attend puts on an elaborate Easter pageant. In it, the devil heckled Jesus on the Mount of Temptation. He also showed up in the crowd as they shouted "Crucify Him!" again and again. Then, once Jesus was dead and buried, Satan and all of his demons stood outside the tomb pushing on the stone. Even though they tried with all of their might to keep the resurrection from happening, they couldn't. All of a sudden there was an explosion. Smoke billowed out as the stone fell on top of the devil, and Jesus triumphantly walked out of the tomb and stood victoriously on top of the stone.

Although this dramatization wasn't literally how it happened, it accurately and symbolically illustrates what's spiritually true. Satan did everything he could, but his power was nothing compared to God's. The resurrection of Jesus Christ is the greatest demonstration of God's power ever!

And you have that same raising-from-the-dead power on the inside of you! It's not out there in heaven somewhere. It's within you—in your born-again spirit. You don't need more power. You just need to believe that you already have it and begin to discover how it operates. Find out the laws that govern how the power of God works and then put them into practice.

If you receive this revelation, it'll ruin you for most of the religious tradition floating around and masquerading as Christianity today.

Commanders, Not Beggars

It'll definitely change the way you pray! You'll stop begging God and saying, "O Lord, I'm nothing. I have nothing, but I believe that You can do anything. Come and move!" Instead, a bold New Testament attitude will cause you to say, "In myself, I am nothing. I don't have any virtue or worth based on my own human ability. But I'm in covenant with You, Father. I am a brand-new creature, and in my born-again spirit, I have the same power that raised Jesus from the dead. You said in Your Word that whomever I lay my hands on will be healed—and I believe it!" Then you'll get up, take your authority, and start commanding and releasing God's power.

This is what Peter did when he looked upon the lame man by the gate of the temple. Realizing God's power within him, Peter declared, "Such as I have give I thee: In the name of Jesus Christ of Nazareth rise up and walk" (Acts 3:6). Then he reached down, grabbed the man by the hand, and lifted him up. The man's feet and ankle bones immediately received strength, and he walked, leaped, and praised God. (Acts 3:7, 8.)

Peter said, "Such as I have." It wasn't his own human strength he was referring to, but God's raising-from-the-dead power within his born-again spirit. Most churches today would kick you out for saying something like that. They'd argue, "You can't do anything!" Of course not—in your physical self. But in the real you—your born-again spirit—you've been given the resurrection life of God!

This understanding will transform you into a commander. No longer will you beg God saying, "The doctor told me I'm going to die, and I can't do anything about it. O God, please heal me!" and then just sit there as a helpless nothing pleading with the Lord to do something. Praying like that shows that you don't yet have the revelation that the same power that raised Jesus Christ is now living on the inside of you. This understanding will change you from being a murmurer, complainer, whiner, and griper into a believer who takes his authority, stands, and demands Satan not to steal what God has given. It's a totally different attitude!

Instead of being petrified and hiding in a corner praying, "God, please get the devil off my back," you'll stand there and say, "Where is he? I just dare Satan to show his ugly face. I'm going to fight him to the death because I have authority and power!" The difference isn't just emotional, but will manifest in your results as well!

Superior Firepower

When I first arrived as a soldier in Vietnam, we came under a heavy attack from the enemy. These weren't guerilla fighters but well-equipped, communist-trained, national troops. Five thousand of them surrounded the mountaintop where only 120 of us U.S. soldiers were stationed. Therefore, we were on "Red Alert." That meant all troops were supposed to stay awake all night and pull bunker guard together instead of taking turns the way we normally did.

That first night I pulled guard all by myself. The other men assigned to that bunker with me fell asleep. I mentioned the Red Alert, but they ignored it. So I stayed up all night by myself. The next night I was too sleepy to do it again, so I became a little more insistent that they stay up with me.

Finally, one of them said, "You must be new." When I responded that I was, they began to laugh. Then they told me how superior our firepower was compared to what the enemy had. If they ever came out of their holes, we would literally wipe them out in minutes. They described to me all the different weapons we had and how powerful they were. During this Red Alert, a "Huey" combat helicopter circled us overhead throughout the night. Just one fifty-caliber "mini-gun" on that helicopter could spray an area the size of a football field with a round every six inches—and the concussion from a fifty-caliber bullet can kill a person if it comes within six inches of their head! The vast superiority of our weapons overwhelmed me. And in a short period of time, I was asleep with the others.

My lack of knowledge is what caused my anxiety in that situation. Once I learned what we had, fear left and confidence came. Of course, I still exercised my alertness, prudence, and wisdom, but now I could rest. Although I wasn't what you'd call "gung-ho" for the war, I thought, *If we must fight, then let's do it on our terms.* I was daring the Enemy to just try and attack us.

So stop whining, griping, complaining, and begging God! Find out what Jesus has already done and learn how to release it. Then confidence will replace fear as you begin acting like the commander you were born again to be!

Majority Rules

Make Paul's prayer your very own, saying, "Father, I have a glimpse of this, but I need a revelation! Open up the eyes of my understanding and help me see the hope of my calling in You. Enlighten me to understand the riches of the glory and the exceeding greatness of Your raising-from-the-dead power that You've placed within my born-again spirit. Father, please give me a revelation of what I already have!"

Not "O God, give me more than I've already got. I don't have enough. I know You can do anything, but I can do nothing." In your carnal self—apart from your born-again spirit—that's true. But you aren't only carnal! Part of you has been born again and now has all of Christ's life, victory, and power already in it.

You are, in your spirit, as Jesus is right now! In your spirit, you are—right at this moment—the same as you'll be throughout all eternity. You don't need God to do something new. You just need a revelation of what He's already done.

You're made up of three distinct parts—spirit, soul, and body. (1 Thess. 5:23.) Your born-again spirit is exactly like God and is always for Him. (Eph. 4:24; 1 Cor. 6:17; 1 John 4:17.) If your soul—your mental, emotional part—becomes renewed and believes what God's Word says is in your spirit, you'll experience the life and power of God within (spirit + soul = 2 against 1). On the other hand, if your soul agrees with your physical body, the life and power of God within you won't be able to manifest in the natural realm (soul + body = 2 against 1). The simple majority always rules!

If you let your sense knowledge dominate you, your soul will agree with your body, and it'll shut off the flow of God's life and power in you. When you let only what you can see, taste, hear, smell, and feel control your thoughts, you'll say, "If I really had the resurrection power of God on the inside of me, I'd feel it. Since I don't feel anything, I must not have it!" That's how the supernatural power of God in your resurrected spirit stays cut off from manifestation.

Wipe Away the Tears

"For I reckon that the sufferings of this present time are not worthy to be compared with the glory which shall be revealed *in* us" (Rom. 8:18, emphasis mine).

Notice that the glory isn't going to be revealed *to* us, but rather *in* us. It's not like we arrive in heaven and then all of a sudden God imparts His glory to us. No, what happens when we arrive in heaven is we'll no longer think carnally. We'll be able to completely see what was already in us!

That's why God will have to wipe the tears away from our eyes. It's not because so many people will just barely make it to heaven. No, it's because when we arrive and receive the full revelation of what we already had, we'll weep, wail, and gnash our teeth over the way we let the devil steal from us. Intimidated by his lies, we begged and pleaded with God to do something He'd already done. Since we didn't believe that He had already done it, we lived far below our privileges in Christ and let the devil beat us up for no good reason. That's why there'll be weeping and wailing at first in heaven. The Lord will have to supernaturally comfort us to enable us to enjoy being there!

This is a totally different mindset. I constantly meet people who are so depressed, discouraged, and defeated that they take offense at what I'm sharing. They think I'm insensitive, uncompassionate, and don't know what it's like to hurt. I'm not going to glorify the devil by listing all of my problems, but I've had things hurt me so bad that I honestly didn't think I could live through the night. I've experienced many things that were beyond my ability to cope with, but here I am alive and well today! These truths I'm sharing with you are what brought me through.

The touchy-feely, feel-good philosophy of the world has permeated into "Christianity" today. Many people would rather sit there and wallow in their pain than get over it. They prefer to receive other's pity, have arms wrapped around them, and get pats on the back, affirming, "Oh yes, it's really miserable," than to come out of it. Some people look more for such momentary "comfort" than they do for the solution that would set them free long-term.

The Answer

What I'm sharing isn't insensitive; it's the answer. It's only the truth you know that will set you free (John 8:32). Your ignorance of God's Word is what Satan uses to keep you in bondage. "My people are destroyed for lack of knowledge" (Hosea 4:6). What you don't know is killing you!

I understand that people have problems. Not everyone believes perfectly or always operates in this. I can have compassion on someone who's fallen into a problem. However, the right reaction when you hear this is: "Father, that's true. Through the death, burial, and resurrection of Jesus Christ, You have already provided everything I need. Right now, it's in my born-again spirit. Therefore, I'm going to get up in the name of Jesus and believe You. I determine in my heart to appropriate what is rightfully mine and to come out of this junk!" Now that's the correct response!

If you just want to keep on hurting and receiving other people's pity, you need to pull your thumb out of your mouth and grow up! Don't just sit there with that sad look on your face. Start recognizing what Jesus has already done for you.

My purpose is to help, not offend. But our passive so-called Christianity today runs so contrary to this truth that many people will be offended by these things I'm saying. However, I challenge you to carefully consider what I'm communicating. Understanding this reality has set me free and enabled me to walk in a higher level of victory than ever before.

I've done things far beyond my mere human ability. I haven't been depressed, discouraged, or defeated in more than thirty-five years. I've seen people raised from the dead, blind eyes opened, and terminal illnesses healed. All of this came through cooperating with the power of God inside me.

Direct From God to You!

What I'm preaching works! It keeps me stable when everything around me seems to be falling apart. If you receive this revelation, it'll work for you too!

Therefore, I encourage you to take this prayer in Ephesians 1:17-23 and combine it with the prayer in Ephesians 3:16-21 and make them your own. Pray them and pray them and pray them—not to make God do something but to open up the eyes of your understanding so that you might see the fullness of what He's already done. Believe me, God wants you to have this revelation even more than you do. Simply open up your heart, start seeking, and become hungry in a positive way, saying, "God, I can't live any longer without a revelation of what You've already done. I refuse to keep asking, begging, and pleading with You to do what You've already done. I must have this understanding!" As you seek Him with all your heart, these truths will totally change your life.

This isn't a revelation you receive once and then never have to revisit. It's the kind of understanding that must become part of your everyday Christian life. The rest of this book will begin to expand and expound on this even further. I believe it'll really help you. But ultimately, you need the Holy Spirit to make this real to you personally. This needs to go beyond mere intellectual knowledge and become revelation knowledge—direct from God to you!

I agree with you now in prayer that the Lord will use these things I've shared to help you receive this revelation that you've already got it!

CHAPTER 5

By Grace Through Faith

The book of Ephesians was written to show you what God has already done. Its prayers don't petition Him for something new, but rather that the eyes of your understanding might be enlightened to see what you already have. (Eph. 1:17, 18.)

Notice how everything is in the past tense:

"And you hath he quickened [made alive], who were dead in trespasses and sins" (Eph. 2:1, brackets mine).

It's not, "You can be quickened if you believe, if you will seek, if you will petition God." No! It's all written from this same "done deal" perspective. You've already got it! God has already quickened you.

Alive!

If you've received Christ, you've been made alive. Although the quickening power of the Lord has been purchased for everyone—Christian and non-Christian alike—the non-Christian hasn't yet received it or been made alive. But as a born-again believer, you have been quickened.

You may not have manifested the life of God in you, but your spirit is as alive as it will ever be. Even though your physical body may be hurting and your soul is still wrestling with depression, your born-again spirit is alive the way Jesus is alive. You have God's resurrection power inside you. You aren't trying to be made alive. You were already made alive in the spirit realm. Through faith, you can draw that life out of your spirit and into your soul and body.

Pray according to God's Word, understanding who you are and what you have in Christ. Don't start petitioning Him from a place of unbelief, opposite the Word, saying, "Lord, I'm dead. There's nothing good in my life. I'm lifeless." Instead say, "Father, I thank You that I do have resurrection life inside of me. The doctor says I'm dying. There's death working in my body, so I'm drawing out Your life which is in me. I thank You that it's done. Now, I take my authority and speak. I command sickness to leave and healing to manifest, in Jesus' name." That's the proper attitude. You've already been quickened!

"Wherein in time past ye walked according to the course of this world, according to the prince of the power of the air, the spirit that now worketh in the children of disobedience" (Eph. 2:2).

Notice how following and being dominated by Satan was something in the past. You might think, *I'm a Christian, but I'm still dominated by the devil.* If that's so, it's because verse 1 isn't reality for you. You don't understand how you've already been quickened and delivered from the death that was in trespasses and sin. When you truly understand that you've been made alive, it breaks the power of sin, and you live in victory.

Your life will be characterized by victory instead of defeat. It's not that you reach sinless perfection and never make a mistake. It's just that when you understand and acknowledge that Christ has already done it—that you already have resurrection life and you are as Jesus is in the spirit—victory is an inevitable byproduct.

"That the communication of thy faith may become effectual [begin to work] by the acknowledging of every good thing which is in you in Christ Jesus" (Philem. 1:6, brackets mine).

Your faith works and you'll see victory manifest—physically, financially, emotionally, etc.—as you acknowledge every good thing in you in Christ!

New Nature / New Seat

"Among whom also we all had our conversation in times past in the lusts of our flesh, fulfilling the desires of the flesh and of the mind; and were by nature the children of wrath, even as others" (Eph. 2:3).

Again, everything is in the past tense. Some say, "But this is still working in me!" If so, it's because you haven't understood that, in the spirit, you already have everything. You are as complete as you'll ever be. Since you haven't understood and acknowledged the good things that are in you in Christ, you're still being dominated by the flesh.

The truth is, your nature has been changed! You don't have an old nature anymore that compels you to live in sin. It died and was buried the moment you accepted Christ. Your new nature—your born-again spirit—was created in righteousness and true holiness.

(Eph. 4:24.) The only reason you still struggle with those old desires toward sin is your unrenewed mind. As God's Word transforms your mind, you'll experience less of those old desires and more of your new nature. (Again, I cover this in much greater detail in my teaching entitled *Spirit, Soul & Body*.)

"But God, who is rich in mercy, for his great love wherewith he loved us, Even when we were dead in sins, hath quickened us together with Christ, (by grace ye are saved)" (Eph. 2:4, 5).

Notice again, it's in the past tense. You've already been quickened. God loved you. He's already done this.

"And hath [past tense] raised us up together, and made us sit together in heavenly places in Christ Jesus" (Eph. 2:6, brackets mine).

This isn't something to seek after or to try to attain unto; it's something to be received as a gift. It's already done. You are already in relationship with God. You are already raised from the dead spiritually and are now seated with Christ in heavenly places.

Sodium & Chloride

"That in the ages to come he might shew the exceeding riches of his grace in his kindness toward us through Christ Jesus. For by grace are ye saved through faith; and that not of yourselves: it is the gift of God: Not of works, lest any man should boast" (Eph. 2:7-9).

That's a powerful passage of Scripture. It's also very familiar. Therefore, many people think they already know what it says.

They just skip over it and don't really give it much time or effort, which is why they don't receive its full benefit.

You were saved by grace through faith. You weren't saved by grace alone. Neither were you saved by faith alone. You were saved by grace through faith. In order to make a point to someone, sometimes I'll emphasize one over the other. For instance, if someone argues, "I believe you have to be holy, pay your tithes, be baptized, etc.," then I'll respond, "No, you're saved by faith. It's your faith in what Jesus did that saves you, not what you do for the Lord." So it's not absolutely wrong to emphasize "you were saved by grace" or "you were saved by faith" in order to make a point. But technically speaking, you weren't saved by grace alone or by faith alone. It was a combination of the two. You were saved by grace through faith!

Grace and faith are like sodium and chloride. If you ingest either one of them alone, it's poisonous. Alone, either one would kill you if taken in a sufficient quantity. However, if you mix them together, you get sodium chloride (table salt). Together, they become something you cannot live without—salt. That's how grace and faith are!

Grace alone (apart from faith) won't save you! In His grace, God has provided salvation for everyone through the death, burial, and resurrection of Jesus Christ. God's grace is the same to everyone. However, not every person is saved. Why? Although the provision for their salvation has already been made (grace), each individual must appropriate God's grace for themselves by faith!

Faith alone (apart from grace) won't save you either! You must put your faith in Jesus Christ and what He accomplished in the atonement (grace). If your faith is in anything else (living holy, paying tithes, reading the Bible, attending church, etc.), it won't produce salvation. Your faith is either in Jesus and what He did (grace) or in yourself and what you do (works). It truly comes down to that! Biblical faith always believes on Jesus and appropriates what God's grace has already provided.

Grace vs. Faith

I'm a grace teacher. I emphasize what God has done for us. Due to this, I've been rejected by many "faith" people. They think I overemphasize God's grace and underemphasize what we must do for God.

I'm also a faith teacher. I emphasize our responsibility to respond positively to what God has already done. That's why I'm rejected by the strong "grace" crowd. They think I put too much emphasis on what we must do.

Overall, the Body of Christ is divided primarily into two different camps—grace or faith. Grace people misunderstand and criticize faith people, and vice versa. Both tend to take their positions to the extreme.

Grace people don't like to hear preaching on faith. Why? They look at it as something we must do. Therefore—to them—it compromises God's grace. They teach that the Christian life is based totally on God's grace. Your faith—what you believe—has nothing to do with it. That's why grace, by itself, will kill you!

On the other hand, faith people don't like to hear preaching on grace. Why? Their focus is all wrapped up in what they must do. They discuss how to build yourself up in faith, what faith will accomplish, etc. Faith preachers don't like to mention God's grace because they feel it weakens people's motivation to be aggressive and make things happen. However, faith, by itself, will also kill you!

All error stems from a truth in God's Word being overemphasized at the expense of other complementary truths. Just take one truth and exalt it to the exclusion of other necessary truths (either through neglect or on purpose), and it'll become an error.

There must be a balance! All truths from God's Word fit together and harmonize. When understood properly, grace and faith complement each other. You were saved by grace through faith. (Eph. 2:8.) It took both, not just one or the other!

Unearned, Undeserved, Unmerited

Grace is multi-faceted. First Peter 4:10 speaks of "the manifold [many-fold, multi-faceted] grace of God" (brackets mine). Therefore, grace can be defined in several different ways.

Most people define *grace* as "unmerited favor." While that's certainly true, it's incomplete. This definition focuses on the truth that grace is unearned and undeserved. It's a gift. If you worked for it, paid for it, or met some minimum requirement in order to receive it—then it wasn't grace. Grace is unearned, undeserved, unmerited favor.

Another important facet of grace is that it's something God did for you, independent of you. By grace, Jesus died for the sins of the entire world. He didn't wait until you'd already lived and sinned before responding to you. No, God accomplished salvation prior to and independent of you. He had predetermined that He would send His Son to the cross for us even before He created the world, before He made people, and before they sinned. Redemption beat in the heart of God long before you came along!

God's grace made the provision for your salvation before you ever needed it. Jesus died for your sins 2,000 years ago—before you were born, before you ever sinned. Prior to and independent of you or anything you could do to earn or deserve it, God provided for your salvation. That's unmerited favor!

Consistent

Grace is also consistent. Since it's not based on our performance, and it's done prior to and independent of any worth, value, or merit on our part, God—by grace—is the same toward everyone. Christian and non-Christian, God-hater and God-lover, His grace is exactly the same.

"For the grace of God that bringeth salvation hath appeared to all men" (Titus 2:11).

Grace includes everything Jesus did for us in the atonement. The Word says His grace has appeared to "all men," not just those who have or will receive it. Therefore, God's grace is the same to everyone.

If grace alone saved you, then everyone would be saved. God's grace is consistent toward all people and has come to all men, but not everyone is saved. Jesus made it very clear that more people will choose the wide gate and broad way leading to destruction than will find the narrow gate leading to life. (Matt. 7:13.) Why? You aren't saved by grace alone. You're saved by grace through faith. You must respond to God's grace with faith in order to receive it.

God extended as much grace toward Adolph Hitler as He has to you or me. But as far as we know, Hitler didn't receive God's grace. Unless Adolph changed his heart at the very last minute, which only God knows, he ended his life resisting the Lord. Even though he was an apparent God-hater, God's grace always remained consistent toward him. But according to our knowledge, Hitler refused to receive it.

God's grace alone doesn't save you. God's grace doesn't heal you by itself. Neither does it bless you. God's grace doesn't do anything for us alone. However, when you receive that grace and mix it with faith, God's power is released to make salvation a reality in your life.

Your Positive Response

Faith is not something you do that makes God move. Studying the Bible, confessing the Word, acting on the Word, etc., are all involved in the faith process, but in themselves they aren't "faith." Faith doesn't make God do anything.

One of the major reasons people aren't receiving more from the Lord is because they think "faith" is God responding to something they do. This puts the burden on you to perform and produce. You may be motivated for a period of time, thinking, *Oh, I'm going to be perfect and do all these things. Then God will heal me.*

Ultimately, nobody can measure up to that. No one's good enough to move God. Faith doesn't move God; He's not stuck. He's not the one who needs to move. Faith is not something you do to make God do something.

The Bible calls such "faith" works and legalism. You're doing something to try to make God do something for you. That's flesh! You can take the Word, confess it, pray, get up, act healed, and throw your medicine away, but your actions will never make God heal you. In fact, works and legalism stop what God has already provided from coming into physical manifestation. Why? God will not be coerced into anything. Everything from God must come by grace through faith!

Faith is simply your positive response to what God has already provided by grace. If what you're calling "faith" is not a response to what God has already done, then it's not true faith. Faith doesn't try to get God to positively respond to you. True faith is your positive response to what God has already done by grace.

Faith only appropriates what God has already provided by grace. If you're trying to make God do something new, then it's not faith. True faith only receives—reaches out and takes—what God has already done.

CHAPTER 6

"Such as I Have"

The early days of the charismatic movement were wild! People met in Bible studies, home groups, and prayer breakfasts because there weren't very many Spirit-filled churches established yet. Mature spiritual oversight was lacking because most of the people involved had just been touched within the last year or two, including the ministers. Therefore, immaturity abounded. Many glorious things happened in the early 1970s, but there was plenty of wildfire too!

Several outstanding scriptures became very popular in those days:

> *Have faith in God. For verily I say unto you, That whosoever shall say unto this mountain, Be thou removed, and be thou cast into the sea; and shall not doubt in his heart, but shall believe that those things which he saith shall come to pass; he shall have whatsoever he saith. Therefore I say unto you, What things soever ye desire, when ye pray, believe that ye receive them, and ye shall have them.*
>
> Mark 11:22-24

And "all things are possible to him that believeth" (Mark 9:23).

According to these verses, whosoever can ask God for whatsoever they desire—and anything's possible! Can you see how easy it would be to slip into error if you didn't know that faith only appropriates what God has already provided by grace?

What Things Soever You Desire?

In my hometown of Arlington, Texas, a woman started a Bible school with twenty or thirty students. She took Mark 11:22-24 and applied it to her desire to be married to Kenneth Copeland. Then she released her faith and began confessing, "I believe I receive, and I shall have it!"

However, Kenneth was already married to Gloria. So this lady viewed Gloria as her "mountain" and began praying for her to "be removed" and "cast into the sea." She actually commanded Gloria to die and get out of the way so she could then marry Kenneth. As an act of her faith, this lady had a wedding ceremony with these Bible college students in attendance where she "married" Kenneth Copeland "in the spirit." Then she just continued waiting for Gloria Copeland to die, so God could put Kenneth and her together.

Thirty-five years have passed, and it hasn't happened yet—and it's not going to either. Why is that, when God's Word plainly says "what things soever ye desire"? Can't you just curse somebody, command them to die, and then marry their spouse? Can't you plan a bank robbery, pray for the money, and then say, "I believe in my heart and confess with my mouth that I'm going to steal a million dollars and not get caught. I believe and receive; it's mine!" Why can't you do those things? It's very simple once you see it.

God—by grace—didn't provide murder, adultery, or thievery in Christ's atonement. Therefore, since Jesus didn't provide it, your "faith" can't make it happen!

Receive What's Already Been Given

Faith doesn't move God. He doesn't respond to what we do "in faith" and then move. By grace, God has already provided everything. The Lord doesn't look at your praying, confessing, begging, fasting, and agreeing with others, and the other things you do as adding up to "enough" to make Him move. Those things aren't like a pry bar that once enough pressure is applied—BOOM—you can make God's power work. The Lord doesn't respond to your faith!

Your faith, if it's a true faith, is simply a response to what He's already done. God—by grace—has already healed everybody. He took upon Himself all of the sins and sicknesses of the entire world at the Cross. He's already dealt with it. It's a done deal. It's over. That's why 1 Peter 2:24 says, "By whose stripes ye *were* [past tense] *healed*" (emphasis and brackets mine). It's already done. The Lord isn't healing people today. He provided healing 2,000 years ago in the death, burial, and resurrection of Christ. People are drawing on that healing by faith and receiving the manifestation of it today. But God already did the necessary work to provide it a long time ago.

Healing was released, transmitted, and broadcast 2,000 years ago in the atonement of the Lord Jesus Christ. Once you're born again, He places within you the same resurrection power that raised Jesus from the dead. It's no longer a matter of getting God to give you healing; He already has. The issue is whether or not you will—by faith—reach out and take it!

When you need healing, God doesn't even have to lift His little finger. People pray, "O God, put forth Your mighty hand." Wrong! The Lord has already accomplished healing and placed it inside your born-again spirit. In order for healing to manifest, you must receive it. You don't have to make God give it; you just have to receive in the physical realm what He's already given you in the spirit. Appropriate—by faith—what God has already provided by grace.

Active Waiting

When you understand what I'm sharing, it'll totally revolutionize the way you receive from God! Most people I minister to are trying to get God to heal them. So they pray, do all these other things, and then passively sit back and wait on Him to move. To justify themselves, they quote scriptures like Psalm 27:14:

> Wait on the LORD: be of good courage, and he shall strengthen thine heart: wait, I say, on the LORD.

They just twiddle their thumbs and sigh, "Well, it's God's turn!" This kind of "waiting" is not how to effectively receive from God.

"Waiting on the Lord" means being like a waiter or a waitress in a restaurant. They aren't just sitting down somewhere, waiting for you to do something. No! When they're waiting on you, they are attentive to you. A good waiter sees when your beverage glass starts getting low and comes right over to fill it.

They are sensitive to and in tune with who they're waiting on, constantly asking, "Is there anything else I can do for you? Are you all right? Do you need anything?" That's the kind of "waiting" the Bible is talking about.

God's Word doesn't advocate waiting on the Lord the way you wait on a bus. It's not a scriptural principle for you to pray and then say, "Well, it's in God's court now. Que sera, sera—whatever will be, will be. It's up to Him. God has seen what I've done, and now we'll see what He'll do." No, God doesn't respond to you!

When a problem comes up in your life, it's nothing new to the Lord. He knew what your problems would be long before you ever had them. By grace, He provided the solution in advance—before you were even born! He provided healing before you ever became sick. He provided joy before tragedy, grief, and sorrow came into your life. God has already made your way of escape. He's already accomplished everything. By grace, it's a done deal! You aren't waiting for God to do something new. He's waiting on you to respond positively to what He's already done!

If you've been believing "God, I've done this, I'm doing that, and I'm confessing these things and waiting for You to heal me," then that's precisely the reason why you aren't seeing healing manifest. It's the wrong attitude! Instead, change your thinking and start saying, "Father, I thank You that You have already healed me. By Your stripes, I was healed. The same power that raised Jesus from the dead is already in me. By faith, I receive what You have already provided!"

"You Command Me!"

Peter didn't even pray a prayer to ask God to heal that man at the temple gate. He just said, "Such as I have, I give it to you!" How could he do that? Peter knew that God had already done it. He understood that God's healing power had already been released. The Lamb had been slain, and the perfect sacrifice had already been made. God—by grace—had already produced healing. Peter didn't wonder, *Will the Lord heal him?* because he knew in his heart that God had already done it.

The only question today is, "Are you ready to believe and receive?" If you're praying for someone else, there needs to be a degree of faith on their part. It's not like it has to be fifty-fifty or something like that. If you're strong in faith, you can carry someone. If they're in neutral, you can at least push them. But if they're in park with the emergency brake on or in reverse fighting against you, saying, "I don't believe God wants it," then you won't be able to make it happen.

When Peter ministered to this man, first he fastened his eyes upon him. (Acts 3:4.) This means he looked at him with a penetrating stare. Paul did the same thing when he ministered to a crippled man in Acts 14:8-10. As he did, he perceived that the man had faith to be healed. (Acts 14:9.) That's exactly what Peter was doing. He perceived this man had enough faith to receive healing if he ministered it to him.

So Peter said, "Such as I have give I thee" (Acts 3:6). When you understand grace—that God has already done everything—you'll become bold and authoritative. You can literally command the power of God to come into manifestation because you aren't commanding God Himself to go and do something. Instead, you're commanding what He has already done to manifest in the physical realm.

When you understand how grace and faith work together, you'll become a commander instead of a beggar. The difference is huge!

"Thus saith the LORD, the Holy One of Israel, and his Maker, Ask me of things to come concerning *my sons,* and *concerning the work of my hands command ye me*" (Isa. 45:11, emphasis mine).

Concerning the work of His hands, God says to His children, "You command Me!"

Flip the Switch!

The power company generates electricity at the power station. Then they deliver it to your house. However, whether your living room light comes on or not has nothing to do with the power company generating electricity. The power is there, but it's been placed at your command. You must go over and flip the switch on the wall. When you do, you're commanding that power to flow.

Since you're the one commanding the power to flow, does that make you stronger than the power company? No! They want you to do it! They've already done their part by generating the electricity, delivering it to your house, and placing it at your command. Flipping the switch doesn't mean you are "forcing" them to do something. All you can "make" them do is what they've agreed to already. You can't make that electricity do something that it's not already wired to do.

You can't force God to do anything that He hasn't—by grace—already done. God (Father & Son Power Company) has already done His part. Through Christ's atonement (the power station), everything you'll ever need has already been generated. In fact, the power has already been delivered to your house (born-again spirit). All you have to do is flip the switch! "Concerning the work of my hands command ye me" (Isa. 45:11). When you believe what He's done and reach out in faith to appropriate it, you're commanding what God has already provided to come into manifestation.

You're the one responsible to flip the switch! If you want your living room light turned on, you can't call the power company and say, "I have people coming over for a party this evening. Could you please turn my living room light on?" They'll answer, "No! The power has already been generated and delivered to your house. We're not going to send someone all the way over there just to turn your living room light on. That's not in our agreement. The power is at your command; you flip the switch!"

God is the power Source, not you. It's His power, not yours. But He's put that power inside your born-again spirit. You didn't produce the power, but it's been placed at your command.

God has already provided everything you need by grace—but it's at your command. Faith positively responds to what God has already done and appropriates it. Faith reaches over into the spiritual realm and draws what God has already supplied, out into the physical realm. If you understand this, it'll revolutionize your life!

Excuses, Excuses

Most people are asking God to do for them what He's already done. They're pleading with Him to give them what He's already given. Then, after praying this way in unbelief, they wonder why they aren't seeing the physical manifestation of their healing. Since they think the Lord can do anything He desires, they wonder, *Why isn't He healing me? If God wanted me well, He could heal me right now!* So they come up with all kinds of excuses like, "God is perfecting me through this trial." Wrong!

For additional light on these important issues, I'd like to recommend some teaching materials. Understanding *Spiritual Authority* will really help you sort these things out. Also, my individual teachings, "The Book of Job," "God's Not Guilty," and "The Sovereignty of God" all soundly debunk this false idea that the Lord puts suffering in your life to teach you things. It's simply not true!

People come up with wrong conclusions like that in order to make sense of their disappointing experience. They pray for healing, thinking that faith is something they do to move God. They believe He evaluates their "faith"—whether they're sincere enough and have done enough—and then He responds to them accordingly. Since there's no apparent response, they wonder, *Why isn't God answering my prayer?* Then they start coming up with different excuses like: "Maybe He's trying to teach me something. Maybe I'm not holy enough. Maybe I haven't prayed enough. Maybe I have sin in my life. Maybe I need to do this and that and all these other things." No—God has already done His part!

When you understand that God has already done it, condemnation is defused. How could you think that you're not holy enough if He's already done it? God provided everything you would ever need before you were born again, before you did anything good or bad, before you were even born! He provided it independent of you—by grace. All you have to do is—by faith—reach over and get it.

Can You Receive?

That's how you were saved! What would have happened if someone had told you that if you'd pray and seek God, beg and plead for mercy, fast and live holy, tithe and be earnest, sincere, and desperate enough, then Jesus would come and die for your sins? If salvation had been presented as something that could happen but hasn't happened yet, the devil could easily have convinced you that "Maybe God can do it and maybe He's done it for others, but He'll never do it for you because you're just too _____ (fill in the blank)."

It's mind-boggling to think that Almighty God would become a human being, take our sicknesses and sin, suffer our punishment, go to hell, and then turn around and give us—as a free gift—salvation. That's too wild! The only way someone could believe that is if it had already happened and the Holy Spirit bore them witness saying, "Yes, I did it! You just have to receive what I've already done for you." If you thought your salvation had yet to be accomplished and was based upon whether or not you were good enough, you'd be convinced, "It won't work for me." But since forgiveness of sins was presented as an already done deal, you were able to receive it.

The same is true of every other salvation benefit, including healing. It's already been provided. At the cross, Jesus bore all your sicknesses, diseases, and infirmities at the same time as He bore all your sin. You don't have to wonder, *Will God heal me?* Like forgiveness, healing is a done deal! It's just a matter of whether you can reach out by faith and receive. If you can get this attitude that healing has already been done, it will manifest. Praise the Lord!

CHAPTER 7

God's Best!

In the early part of 2000, I ministered on grace and faith at a church in Lewisville, Texas. It's the same truth I've taught thousands of times (in book form as "Living in the Balance of Grace and Faith"). I emphasized how faith works and countered some common misconceptions (i.e., "faith" is believing God to do something in the future). While sharing that true Bible faith is believing what God has already done by grace, I used healing as my main example.

Chris Ochenski attended that meeting and took a tape of the message home to her sick daughter. Niki loved the Lord and enjoyed a close relationship with Him. However, at age nineteen, she had been very ill for five long years.

Misdirected Faith

Niki was believing God for her healing but hadn't received the manifestation yet. She'd seen visions of the Lord, and in them He told her that she would be healed. Because of this, she had faith and was happy. Niki was praising God even though her doctor—

who kept a weekly appointment with her—never expected to see her alive again. Niki was nearly gone!

Although she had faith, it was misdirected. Niki believed God was—future tense—going to heal her. She was passively waiting on the Lord to do something. Then she listened to my message on cassette about how God has already done it and faith just reaches over to appropriate what's already been provided. My statement "Progressive miracles aren't God's best!" really upset Niki at first.

I'm not against progressive miracles, and there's no "bad" way to be healed. However, some ways are definitely better than others—and God's best for everyone is always an instantaneous miracle! The only reason progressive miracles come is because of the way people believe. Their theology—the way they think—only lets it manifest a little at a time.

Since the Lord had told her that she would have a progressive miracle, Niki took offense at my remark. But because she had such a good relationship with God, she just asked Him about it. While listening to the tape, she said in her heart, "Now, God, what about that? You told me I was going to be healed progressively!" He answered saying, "Niki, that's according to your faith. That's what you were believing for. It was all you could receive, so I was meeting you where you were. But My best is instantaneous!"

Once she understood, Niki saw that she could've been healed five years before. She'd been passively "waiting" on God, and her faith wasn't out there for an instantaneous healing. She hadn't understood how grace and faith work together to bring into manifestation what God has already provided. This became a revelation to her as she recognized her healing was already done.

Redirected Faith

The next day, I went over to the Ochenskis' house. I was praying that Niki would become so angry that she'd reach out in aggressive, violent faith and take her healing. (Matt. 11:12.) Up until then, she hadn't been able to feed herself, go to the bathroom on her own, or even brush her hair. Niki wasn't paralyzed, but she was so weak and frail that she couldn't even lift her hand—much less move, walk, or do anything. However, after I arrived, Niki became so riled up that she put her arm across my chest, pushed me out of the way, stood up, and walked!

All I did was redirect her faith! Niki had thought that "faith" was something she did, and sooner or later God would respond and grant healing. I simply told her, "No, that's not Bible faith. You must believe that God has already done it. Then—by faith—reach over into the spirit realm and take what's rightfully yours!" Healing manifested—BOOM—just as soon as Niki received the revelation!

This ministered to me too! I saw how this understanding could effectively redirect a person's faith. Therefore, I've been trying to share it with as many people as I can. Since Niki's healing was so dramatic in illustrating this truth, we made a video out of it called "Niki Ochenski: The Story of a Miracle!" This powerful video has already impacted tens of thousands of lives!

I've seen more individuals healed in the past few years than I have in a long, long time. It's simply because people are understanding and saying, "I'm no longer asking God to heal me; I am receiving my healing, which He has already provided. When I pray for people, I'm no longer asking God to heal them. Instead, I'm ministering healing. I'm giving them healing—the same healing virtue that God has placed in me!" Both myself, and others, are seeing infinitely better results—glory to God!

Reach Out and Receive!

All of this applies to your financial prosperity too! God has already commanded blessing and the power to get wealth upon you. You just have to learn how to reach out in faith and receive it!

God doesn't give you wealth directly; He gives you power to get it instead.

"But thou shalt remember the LORD thy God: for it is he that giveth thee power to get wealth, that he may establish his covenant" (Deut. 8:18).

As a born-again believer, you already have God's wealth anointing and prosperity power. However, you must believe in your heart that you already have it and then put it to work by faith.

Many things are involved in the process of putting this power to work and seeing wealth manifest. You need to whole-heartedly seek God and His kingdom first. (Matt. 6:33.) You must trust in Him and start giving. It's important to understand that there's always a period of time between sowing and reaping. Also, you must go out and work. There are many, many practical things you can do to actively cooperate with God's laws of faith concerning prosperity.

The Lord has worked these truths deep into my life. My wife and I have gone from nearly starving to death on several occasions as impoverished young ministers to seeing God provide an average of $1,200 every hour of every day of the year for the purpose of preaching the Gospel. I have several teachings that will help you better understand and receive the manifestation of prosperity, including: "Grace and Faith in Giving," *Financial Stewardship, Blessings and Miracles,* and *The Power of Partnership.* Prosperity is simply having enough of God's supply to fully accomplish His will for your life. I pray that you get a hold of this revelation and fully accomplish your destiny in Him!

Once you believe that God—by grace—has already provided prosperity, you'll begin to reach out in faith and take it. You'll start cooperating with the power and anointing to get wealth that is already in your born-again spirit. Instead of just praying and asking God to dump a bunch of money in your lap while you sit at home watching "As the Stomach Turns" on television, you'll get up, go out, and start touching things. Why? Because you know that God has promised to bless all the work of your hands! (Deut. 28:8, 12.)

When you start doing things—believing for that anointing to manifest and prosperity to come—then you'll start seeing it. If you just sit at home, pray, and wait for God to magically put money in your wallet, you'll never receive it. God said He'd bless the work of your hands. One hundred times zero is zero ($100 \times 0 = 0$). You need to believe that God has already done His part, and then do something. It's not, "God, did You see that I worked? Now, release Your power!" No! You're working because you believe that God has already given you this anointing to get wealth, and you're acting in faith to release that power to manifest the prosperity the Lord has already provided. Can you see the difference?

God Has Already Moved

Confession doesn't make God move. You're wrong if you think reciting "By His stripes I am healed" 599 times will force God to heal you. You can't make God do anything! Faith doesn't move Him. God—by grace—has already moved as much as He's going to. He's already provided everything. Your need was abundantly supplied before you even had it. Since the Lord has already done it, you confess God's Word to encourage your own heart and to drive off the devil. It might take you confessing that Word 599 times before you actually believe (Rom. 10:17), but God's not the one who needs to move; He already has. Confession moves you into faith and the devil out of the way so your manifestation can come. (Rev. 12:11.)

You don't have to read the Bible to make God love you! He won't love you any more than He already does if you read the Word, and neither will He love you any less. However, you'll love God more if you read the Bible, and you'll love Him less if you don't. His love doesn't change; yours does. God has put things in His Word that draw out this love and everything else He's already placed in your life.

Living holy doesn't make God love you more. Neither does a lack of holiness cause Him to love you less. God—by grace—is the same toward everyone. However, if you don't live holy, you won't love God as much. Through sin, your heart will become hard, and you'll deaden yourself to the things of God. (Heb. 3:13.)

You need to study the Word, fellowship with believers, and do good things, but not in order to move God. He's already moved, but you recognize that you must—by faith—reach over into the spiritual realm and receive. Attending church, reading the Word, and listening to good Bible teaching doesn't cause God to move in your life; they help your faith!

Even reading this book won't make God love you more. He isn't going to look down on you and say, "You read Andrew's book! I'm giving you three stars. At six stars, you'll get one answered prayer!" No, that's not how He works! The Lord loves you, and His grace is the same toward you whether or not you read this book. However, you won't be the same toward God and His grace without this understanding. Apart from this revelation, you won't have the same degree of faith operating in your life. This teaching is helping your faith—your positive response to what God has already done.

Reading the Bible and going to church help you. Studying the Word and fellowshipping with other believers stir your love for God. (Heb. 10:23-25.) However, the Lord would love you exactly the same if you never went to church or read the Word again. But that's stupid! Why would you cut yourself off from the very things God's given to help you walk by faith?

Faith Responds to Grace

Although you need to do those things, don't ever think that your actions make God react. He never reacts to us. God has already done everything by grace, and faith is our reaction to Him. Flesh, works, and legalism all try to do things in order to solicit a positive response from God. But the Lord said He'd never share His glory with anyone. You didn't "make" God save, heal, or prosper you. He had already done it. All you did was respond positively in faith to reach out and appropriate what He had already provided.

Don't confuse trying to "make" God do something with your faith causing what He's already done to manifest. You can't force God to do anything. But—by faith—you can make what He's already provided to manifest. That's a big difference!

Faith is simply your positive response to what God has already done. You don't get the glory. You can't say that you made something happen. It was God's power, not yours. He wasn't reacting to you or anything you've done. You simply responded to His grace!

Faith or grace taken alone—apart from the other—will kill you! They must complement each other in order for you to experience the abundant life God intended for you to enjoy. Faith teaching, if it's just "Do something to move God!" will kill you. You'll end up stuck in the flesh—frustrated, legalistic, and works-oriented. On the other hand, extreme grace will also kill you. If it's, "God does everything and you have nothing to do with it," your subsequent passivity will prevent what the Lord has done from manifesting in your life. Then you'll have to make up all kinds of excuses for why you aren't experiencing the abundant life God provided by His grace and clearly promised in His Word. Grace and faith must work together!

"I Labored More Abundantly"

Paul understood and lived by this truth.

"But by the grace of God I am what I am: and his grace which was bestowed upon me was not in vain; but I laboured more abundantly than they all: yet not I, but the grace of God which was with me" (1 Cor. 15:10).

Paul cooperated with God's grace. He didn't labor in order to get it, but once grace came, he labored in faith to reach out and receive what God had already done. That's a powerful revelation!

I pray that God gives you understanding and wisdom as you begin to harmonize this revelation of grace and faith and apply it to your daily life. The rest of this book will build upon the foundation that's been laid thus far. I'll be sharing some things that will really encourage and help you to successfully walk this out.

CHAPTER 8

Seeing in the Spirit

We're already blessed. (Eph. 1.) God has already done it. He's already blessed us with every spiritual blessing in Christ. (Eph. 1:3.) We have the same power that raised Jesus Christ from the dead living on the inside of us. (Eph. 1:19, 20.) Everything we'll ever need has already been provided. It's not a matter of asking God to do it, but rather believing that it's already done and releasing it to manifest.

God—by grace—has already done everything. Faith isn't something we do to make God move. Rather, it's our positive response to what He's already done. Since God has already done it, faith is simple; it's not a struggle. We don't have to do all these things in order to twist God's arm. Faith is simply our responding in a positive way to what God has already done.

"How Can This Be?"

Many people wonder, *How can this be?* It's like their circuits overload and start to blow. They say, "I'm miserable and fighting depression. I don't understand how you can say that the Lord has already done everything He's going to do and I'm already healed.

That can't be right. Here's my doctor's report. This proves that wrong!" Or they feel pain and other symptoms in their bodies and conclude, "Nope, I'm not healed." For many people, these truths are simply beyond belief because they're so obviously contrary to what they're presently experiencing in the physical realm.

Yet the Bible clearly teaches that God has already blessed you. You have the same power that raised Jesus Christ from the dead. Everything's a done deal, and you've already got it. So you're probably wondering, *If all this is true, then where is it?* In the spirit realm!

God has already moved and blessed us with every spiritual blessing. Everything we'll ever need—joy, peace, wisdom, revelation knowledge, etc.—has already been provided. But it's all in the spirit realm.

If you can't understand that everything God has already provided for you is in the spirit realm, then you'll lose this truth I'm communicating. Why? Because the physical realm does not exactly reflect what's true in the spirit realm. Faith acts like a bridge to bring what is true and real in the spiritual world into the physical world. The truth is, very few believers allow their faith to be that bridge for what God has already done to cross over into the natural realm. We just don't see very much manifestation of it.

My New Identity

One of the first things the Lord gave me a clear revelation of was the truth that I'd become righteous. It wasn't a righteousness I had earned through my works, but rather a free gift He gave me based upon His work. (2 Cor. 5:21.) It didn't come from my living holy and doing everything right. When I was born again, Jesus Christ Himself became my righteousness. (1 Cor. 1:30.) My born-again spirit was "created in righteousness and true holiness" (Eph. 4:24). My new nature was created to be righteous. It's not something I'm becoming or evolving into. In my spirit, I am righteous. So is every other born-again believer!

I saw this truth in the Word and in my heart, but I couldn't perceive it in my experience. I looked in the mirror and saw zits, wrinkles, and bulges. My feelings and thoughts included anger, bitterness, lust, and many other nasty things at times. In considering all of this, I knew I wasn't being like Jesus. At the time, I thought that when the Bible spoke of being righteous—in right standing with God—it meant sinless perfection in my thoughts, feelings, and actions. So I diligently searched my physical actions (body), and my thoughts and my feelings (mental-emotional realm, a.k.a. the soul), but I still couldn't perceive this righteousness. I really struggled with this for a long period of time. Then the Lord gave me revelation concerning spirit, soul, and body. (For further study, see *Spirit, Soul & Body*).

Through this revelation of spirit, soul, and body, I realized that when the Bible calls me righteous, it's talking about my born-again spirit—not my thoughts, feelings, actions, and physical body. I began to understand that in my spirit, I was totally changed. I'm a new creature. There's a new me!

"Therefore if any man be in Christ, he is a new creature: old things are passed away; behold, all things are become new" (2 Cor. 5:17).

I started to recognize that in my spirit, I had become a totally brand-new person!

When I stopped going by what I saw in the mirror, thought in my mind, and observed in my actions, I began to experience victory in my Christian life. As I changed my identity to who the Word said I was in the spirit, I started enjoying the promised abundant life in manifestation. (John 10:10.) How did that happen? Through God's Word!

"So Are We in This World"

God's Word is the only reliable, accurate representation of the spirit world. Jesus declared:

"It is the spirit that quickeneth [makes alive]; the flesh profiteth nothing: the words that I speak unto you, they are spirit, and they are life" (John 6:63, brackets mine).

God's Word is spiritual. The Bible tells us what's truly going on in the spirit realm.

That's why some people struggle so much to understand God's Word. They're trying to perceive in the natural realm what the Bible is speaking of in their spirit! Take, for instance, 1 John 4:17: "As he [Jesus Christ] is, so are we in this world" (brackets mine). It's not talking about your physical actions (body) or your thoughts and feelings (soul), because God's Word plainly reveals that someday (future—when you arrive in heaven), your body and soul (corruptible) will complete the process of change to perfection (will put on incorruption). (1 Cor. 13:9-12, 15:50-54.) However, Christ is perfect right now. So then, what part of you is already perfect—as Jesus is? Your born-again spirit!

As Jesus is—right at this moment—so are you in this world. It's not talking about when you get to heaven. It means right now here on earth. You can't say you're acting exactly as Jesus. You might be acting better than me, or better than you've ever acted before, but you're not manifesting everything physically, emotionally, and mentally exactly as Jesus is. The only way to understand 1 John 4:17 is to realize that it's talking about your born-again spirit. In the spirit, you're a totally brand-new person. The real you—who you'll be throughout eternity— is who you are in Christ. Living from who you are in Christ is what the Word calls "walking by the spirit" (Gal. 5:16). If you begin to do that, then you'll find the power of God manifest in your life.

The Spiritual Mirror

God's Word is a spiritual mirror. When you look into it, you see who you are in the spirit. (2 Cor. 3:18.) It always reflects "Christ in you, the hope of glory" (Col. 1:27). This shines additional light on James 1:22-25 (brackets mine):

> But be ye doers of the word, and not hearers only, deceiving your own selves. For if any be a hearer of the word, and not a doer, he is like unto a man beholding his natural face in a glass [mirror]: For he beholdeth himself, and goeth his way, and straightway forgetteth what manner of man he was. But whoso looketh into the perfect law of liberty [the Word, especially the New Testament], and continueth therein, he being not a forgetful hearer, but a doer of the work, this man shall be blessed in his deed.

As you look in the mirror (God's Word), discover your identity in Christ (who you are in the spirit), and act on that knowledge in faith, you'll see the life of God within you manifest.

If I told you your hair was messed up, how would you know if it was or not? You can't go by how it feels. The only way you can know is to look in a mirror. Then you just believe it and act accordingly. If some hairs are out of place, you comb them. You trust the mirror to tell you the truth.

However, what you see in a mirror is only a reflection; it's not the real thing. You've never really seen your face before. It's true; think about it! You might have observed your reflection in a mirror, viewed a photograph, or seen a drawing, but you've never looked directly at your own face. How do you know that these representations of your face are accurate? Haven't you seen those funny mirrors at a circus or carnival? Everyone knows that they "doctor" those pictures of people in magazines at the grocery store, and drawing caricatures is even considered a form of art. Therefore, you have to trust that the image you're seeing in the mirror is true.

It's the same when you look into the spiritual mirror of God's Word. The Word tells you who you are and what you have in Christ. It reveals spiritual truths and what's happening in the spiritual world. If you want to experience life and peace, then you need to be spiritually minded.

"For to be carnally [not necessarily sinfully, but naturally] minded is death; but to be spiritually minded is life and peace" (Rom. 8:6, brackets mine).

You'll never move into the supernatural things of God while being dominated by the natural realm—what you can see, taste, hear, smell, and feel. If you can't believe anything beyond what your five senses can tell you or confirm, then you are carnally minded. If something must be proven in a test tube, scientifically, before you'll believe it exists, then you're trapped in the natural realm. God is a Spirit, and He moves in the spirit realm. (John 4:24.) In order to flow with God in the supernatural and enjoy life and peace, you need to become spiritually minded.

CHAPTER 9

The Spirit Realm Is Real

Some people see what God has done in the Scriptures, but then they run into this wall. "The Word says I already have everything, but I don't look blessed, I don't feel healed, and it sure doesn't seem like I have the power and anointing of God. There's no tingling in my hands or anything! How can you say that I can heal the sick, raise the dead, and so forth?" It's in the spirit, not the physical realm. These are two different worlds.

In 2 Kings 6, the king of Syria was warring against the king of Israel. He would send ambushes out to destroy the king of Israel's army. However, every time he did this, an ambush would be there waiting for him. It was as if the king of Israel knew the king of Syria's battle plans beforehand.

After this happened a number of times, the king of Syria was quite perplexed.

"Therefore the heart of the king of Syria was sore troubled for this thing; and he called his servants, and said unto them, Will ye not shew me which of us is for the king of Israel?" (2 Kings 6:11).

Basically, he asked, "Who's the traitor? Someone here must be a spy!"

"And one of his servants said, None, my lord, O king: but Elisha, the prophet that is in Israel, telleth the king of Israel the words that thou speakest in thy bedchamber" (2 Kings 6:12).

Elisha, who was listening to God, kept telling the king of Israel what was going on. The king trusted what the prophet was seeing and hearing in the spirit, and acted on his counsel. Therefore, he was able to defeat the Syrian army every single time.

Spiritual Truth vs. Physical Truth

So the king of Syria decided to pursue Elisha.

Therefore sent he thither horses, and chariots, and a great host: and they came by night, and compassed the city about [where Elisha was]. And when the servant of the man of God was risen early, and gone forth, behold, an host compassed the city both with horses and chariots. And his servant said unto him, Alas, my master! how shall we do?

2 Kings 6:14, 15, brackets mine

That's just an old English way of saying he panicked.

This man saw the armies, discerned why they were there, and panicked! He knew his master, Elisha, had been giving the king of Syria's battle plans to the king of Israel. But notice the prophet's response:

"Fear not: for they that be with us are more than they that be with them" (2 Kings 6:16).

Now, people who don't understand that there's more to life than what you can see, taste, hear, smell, and feel would look at Elisha here and say, "He lied!" To them, there's simply no reality beyond the physical realm. Therefore, they don't understand people who are operating in faith. They think a believer is just saying that they're healed—when they really aren't—in the hope that it'll become so. I once heard a man preach, "You have to say it's so when it isn't so in order for it to become so." Not true! That's just lies, deception, and mind games. The faith person is simply describing what's true in the spirit but hasn't yet manifested in the physical realm.

You need to realize that spiritual truth and physical truth don't always agree. However, if you'll believe, speak, and act on spiritual truth, it'll overcome the physical truth. Your unwavering faith in God's eternal Word causes the contrary temporal realm to change. That's how what's already true in the spirit becomes true in the physical.

A person who's genuinely operating in faith confesses what God has already done in the spirit. That's how a person's telling the truth when he says, "I am blessed! I have everything I need. I'm a prosperous person," even though his checkbook is in the red. That's how someone can declare, "By His stripes, I was healed. I've already been healed. Thank You, Jesus!" when her body is wracked with pain and other symptoms. She's not just "fakin' it 'til she makes it." As she continues to believe, what's true in the spirit will eventually manifest itself in the physical realm.

That's what Elisha did! He declared, "Fear not: for they that be with us are more than they that be with them" (2 Kings 6:16). The prophet would have been lying if all there was to reality was just this physical world—what you can see, taste, hear, smell, and feel. But, of course, there's a real spiritual realm.

"Lord, Open His Eyes"

However, Elisha's servant wasn't operating in faith the way his master was. Apparently, the prophet's confident answer shocked him. So Elisha prayed:

"LORD, I pray thee, open his eyes, that he may see. And the LORD opened the eyes of the young man; and he saw: and, behold, the mountain was full of horses and chariots of fire round about Elisha" (2 Kings 6:17).

The young man's physical eyes were already wide open. I bet they were as big as saucers, seeing all of those Syrians there to take them! But God opened the eyes of his heart so he could see in the spirit. That's what enabled him to perceive all of the horses and chariots of fire round about them!

You have the ability to see the unseen. Don't limit yourself only to what you can perceive with your natural eyes. Through God's Word, look beyond just the mere physical world. With the eyes of your heart you can see in the spirit!

Jesus used this same reasoning when He said, "He that hath ears to hear, let him hear" (Matt. 11:15). Every person listening had physical ears on their head and heard what He was saying. But Jesus was referring to those who would hear Him with their hearts and receive His words into their innermost beings.

In order to walk with God and do exploits, you need to be able to perceive things in your heart that you cannot perceive with your five natural senses. This is what Elisha prayed for his servant. God answered and the man's spiritual eyes opened up to see the many angels surrounding them.

When the servant saw them was not when the angels arrived. They were already there. He just wasn't aware of it.

Believing Is Seeing

The Word gives us no indication that Elisha had his eyes opened too. He didn't see this, because he didn't need to. He believed it based on the promises of God.

God had already given many promises by that time. David was a prophet before then and had written many things, including:

"For he shall give his angels charge over thee, to keep thee in all thy ways. They shall bear thee up in their hands, lest thou dash thy foot against a stone" (Ps. 91:11, 12).

There were many other promises about angels too. Plus, Elisha had physically seen the horses and chariots of God before. (2 Kings 2:11, 12.) Apparently, Elisha just believed. He didn't have to see.

As believers we have many spiritual truths and realities in and around us that most of us have never perceived. Dominated by carnal-mindedness, we limit what we believe to what we can perceive with our five natural senses. We must go beyond the physical realm and begin to recognize that there's a real spiritual world!

In the spirit, God has already healed you. He's already commanded His blessing upon you. You've been given joy, peace, and love. All of these things, and so much more, are in you in abundance—in your born-again spirit. But before you see these things on the outside (physically manifest), you must see them on the inside (with the eyes of your heart).

The spiritual world is not fake. It's not a fantasyland. It's reality! In fact, the spiritual world actually created the physical world. Everything we can see and touch—the visible—was created by the invisible.

"Through faith we understand that the worlds were framed by the word of God, so that things which are seen were not made of things which do appear" (Heb. 11:3).

God took spiritual substance—things that were real in the spiritual realm—and made everything in the physical realm. The spiritual realm is the parent force, and the parent force is always greater. The Creator is always greater than the creation. From God's eternal point of view, the spiritual realm is more real than the natural.

Elisha understood this. Since he believed he had angelic protection surrounding him, he boldly walked out into the midst of the enemy, raised his hand, and smote them with blindness. They immediately began groping around in their darkness. Elisha commanded them to take each other's hands and led them single file directly to the king of Israel. Then he prayed and their eyes were opened. (2 Kings 6:18-20.) Elisha took the entire Syrian army captive because he believed in the power that was available to him in the spirit realm. He knew it was there and drew upon it. Elisha didn't use a single natural weapon to accomplish this—only spiritual. The spirit realm is real!

CHAPTER 10

Where God Moves

Daniel also clearly exemplifies the reality of the spiritual realm. He prayed to receive revelation knowledge concerning Jeremiah's prophecy, which at the time appeared to not be coming to pass. (Dan. 9:2.)

"And this whole land shall be a desolation, and an astonishment; and these nations shall serve the king of Babylon seventy years" (Jer. 25:11).

More than seventy years had already come and gone. However, the Lord showed Daniel later in the chapter that this was really seventy weeks of years (490 years), not seventy years. (Dan. 9:24.)

So Daniel asked for this revelation and began to pray.

"And I set my face unto the Lord God, to seek by prayer and supplications, with fasting, and sackcloth, and ashes: And I prayed unto the LORD my God, and made my confession, and said..." (Dan. 9:3, 4).

His prayer continues down through verse 19:

"O Lord, hear; O Lord, forgive; O Lord, hearken and do; defer not, for thine own sake, O my God: for thy city and thy people are called by thy name."

Three Minutes

And whiles I was speaking, and praying, and confessing my sin and the sin of my people Israel, and presenting my supplication before the LORD my God for the holy mountain of my God; Yea, whiles I was speaking in prayer, even the man Gabriel [the same angel who appeared to Zacharias and Mary in Luke 1:19, 26-28], whom I had seen in the vision at the beginning, being caused to fly swiftly, touched me about the time of the evening oblation. And he informed me, and talked with me, and said, O Daniel, I am now come forth to give thee skill and understanding.

Daniel 9:20-22, brackets mine

It took Daniel about three minutes to pray this prayer. (Dan. 9:4-19.) While he was still praying, the angel Gabriel showed up and announced, "I've come with your answer!" Wouldn't it be wonderful if everything you prayed for manifested itself in three minutes?

Notice when it was that God actually answered:

"*At the beginning of thy supplications the commandment came forth,* and I am come to shew thee; for thou art greatly beloved: therefore understand the matter, and consider the vision" (Dan. 9:23, emphasis mine).

God moved in the spiritual world and gave the commandment at the very beginning of Daniel's prayer, yet it took approximately three minutes for Gabriel to show up!

Why Not Instantaneous Manifestation?

Most people assume that God doesn't have to deal with such things as time, space, or distance. However, this is a clear biblical example where God gave a command to one of His angels, and it took approximately three minutes for him to show up. That's not a long period of time, but it plainly reveals that God moved in the spiritual realm before there was any physical evidence of it.

Most people believe that when God wills something to happen, the very moment He thinks it—BOOM—there's instantaneous manifestation in the natural realm. They don't think the Lord has to deal with any restrictions or limits. However, this example shows God giving the command and it taking approximately three minutes.

The Bible doesn't explain what was happening during that brief period of time. Maybe Gabriel needed to pack. Maybe he was on the other side of the universe and it took him three minutes to cover a hundred billion light years. Who knows what was going on. But it establishes the principle that God commanded it in the spirit realm before there was physical manifestation.

Daniel prayed again in chapter 10. If anything, his heart should have been encouraged and his faith strengthened after receiving such a powerful and relatively quick answer in chapter 9. Although the same man prayed, the results were much different!

Demonic Opposition

I like using Daniel as an example of how God answers prayer. If I illustrated this point with an example from my life, you'd be tempted to dismiss it saying, "Well, Andrew, you're different from me. You must be one of God's favorites. Some people He just responds to better than others." You can't say that about Daniel! This same man prayed and received two totally different results.

This time it took three weeks—not three minutes—before Daniel saw the manifestation of what he prayed for.

"In those days I Daniel was mourning three full weeks. I ate no pleasant bread, neither came flesh nor wine in my mouth, neither did I anoint myself at all, till three whole weeks were fulfilled" (Dan. 10:2, 3).

Daniel fasted and prayed again, but the results were worse, not better.

> And, behold, an hand touched me, which set me upon my knees and upon the palms of my hands. And he said unto me, O Daniel, a man greatly beloved, understand the words that I speak unto thee, and stand upright: for unto thee am I now sent. And when he had spoken this word unto me, I stood trembling.
>
> Daniel 10:10, 11

Why does God answer some prayers in three minutes and others in three weeks? Have you ever wondered about this? Have you ever seen God do something quickly for you and on other occasions take weeks, months, even years? Through all that time you stood, believed, and wondered, *God, why are You doing this? What's taking You so long to answer my prayer?* That's actually an invalid question. The next verse shows why.

"Then said he unto me, Fear not, Daniel: for *from the first day* that thou didst set thine heart to understand, and to chasten thyself before thy God, *thy words were heard,* and I am come for thy words" (Dan. 10:12, emphasis mine).

God gave the command and answered the very first day, but it didn't manifest until three weeks later. Why? There was demonic opposition!

"But the prince of the kingdom of Persia [a demonic power] withstood me one and twenty days [three weeks]: but, lo, Michael, one of the chief princes [another angel; see Jude 9 and Rev. 12:7], came to help me; and I remained there with the kings of Persia" (Dan. 10:13, brackets mine).

Three weeks and additional help were required for this angelic messenger to break through the demonic opposition and manifest Daniel's answer!

Things That Hinder

God moved instantly both times. It wasn't that He answered in three minutes the first time and three weeks the second. God answered Daniel's prayer immediately on both occasions. God wasn't the variable. He didn't change. God remained constant. In the Old Covenant, Daniel was looking forward in faith to what Jesus would do. Today, as New Testament believers, we look back to what God has already done through Christ. It's a done deal!

God doesn't answer some prayers in three minutes and others in three weeks. The Lord answers everything immediately! The supply is already there. It's already been done. The provision was made before you ever had the need. It's not God moving differently for different people. Rather, it's people who receive differently. God has already done His part, but there are things that hinder what He's done in the spiritual realm from coming into the physical world.

Many people wrongly assume that the devil is all-powerful and all-knowing. Functionally, they believe that Satan is more faithful than God! They aren't sure if the Lord will answer their prayer, even if they do everything just right. But they're absolutely convinced that the devil will devour them if they do even one little thing wrong. They think the devil is always there and never misses a trick. "The enemy's doing this and Satan's doing that. He's saying this and saying that. Blah, blah, blah!"

You need to recognize that there's only one devil, and he's not omnipresent. He can only be in one place at a time. So for every believer to say that Satan has personally spoken to and tempted us each and every day is absolutely incorrect. Sure, the kingdom of darkness is against us, but we give the devil too much credit. He's not all-powerful. He doesn't always do things right.

It's very possible that the devil missed it in Daniel 9. Perhaps he was out licking his wounds, sulking and pouting, and misjudged how dangerous Daniel was. Maybe Satan was on vacation. Maybe he was tired and sleeping. We give the devil too much recognition. Anyone who fights against God sure isn't bright. I'm not saying he's stupid, just that he misses it sometimes.

The Variable

So in chapter 9, Daniel's prayer got through to God, and Gabriel appeared with the answer in three minutes. Satan wasn't even a factor! But after Daniel received such a powerful revelation and prophesied several important elements concerning the Messiah, the devil marshaled his forces to make sure Daniel didn't pray unopposed ever again.

Satan—not God or Daniel—was the variable. Sometimes he fights us, sometimes he doesn't. I don't know all the reasons for this, but we give the devil way too much credit when we think he's consistent and always does things right. Satan blows it lots of times!

Scripture gives no indication that demons reproduce and have baby demons. Therefore, it's safe to say that the number of evil spirits working on the earth hasn't grown over the centuries and millennia. Either there was a huge number of demons per person back in Adam and Eve's day, or there's a lack of demons today. There are at least six billion people on the planet now. If everyone has a personal demon, then back in the early days there must have been six billion of them attacking Adam, Eve, and their children. However, if there aren't that many to begin with, then today there's a shortage of demons to go around. Personally, I don't believe the devil can do everything he tries to do. He's not limitless in his ability to fight us. I think Satan just lets some people go because he's shorthanded.

So Daniel, for whatever reason, got his prayer through to God without resistance in chapter 9, but Satan hindered his prayer in chapter 10. When most believers pray today and don't see their answer immediately manifest, they get mad at God and wonder what's going on. Instead of saying, "O God, I've prayed and nothing's happened. When will You answer me?" pray, "Father, I know You are faithful. Thank You for answering me. I know it's almost manifest!" Don't lose your faith just because you've been waiting three weeks for the manifestation!

The Bridge

What would have happened if Daniel had moved out of faith and quit praying on the twentieth day in chapter 10? He easily could have reasoned, *Well, God answered my prayer last time in three minutes. By this time tomorrow, it'll have been three whole weeks. I quit!* If Daniel had done that, his answer wouldn't have manifested. Even though God had already given the commandment and the messenger was on his way, the demonic opposition would have prevailed had Daniel withdrawn his faith.

God does things according to the power that's at work in us. (Eph. 3:20.) That's why we must believe! Faith is the bridge that God's provision uses to cross out of the spirit realm into the physical. We must provide that bridge. God is a Spirit, and He moves in the spirit world. (John 4:24.) Whether what's spiritually true ever manifests itself in the natural realm or not isn't dependent upon God answering prayer, but whether we can—by faith— reach over into the spiritual realm and bring what He's already done into physical manifestation. Our faith provides the bridge for God to cross over into the physical world.

God doesn't do things without us, and we certainly can't do anything without Him. God is the One who must provide something in the first place in the spirit. But then He flows through us to get it into the natural realm. That's an awesome revelation!

Authority + Power = Responsibility

Daniel persevered in prayer. He may or may not have under-stood all of these things, but he knew God had his answer and simply refused to quit until it manifested. Prior to the angel's arrival and explanation, the Word doesn't indicate that Daniel knew what was happening in the spiritual world as he prayed. From his perspective, it may have seemed like God was totally silent and ignoring him. Yet Daniel persevered and continued praying in faith. However, even if God had shown him that a demonic power was hindering the messenger from bringing his answer, Daniel couldn't have done anything about it. Why? Old Testament saints didn't have any power or authority over the devil.

As a New Testament believer, God has given you authority and power. With that comes responsibility.

"Submit yourselves therefore to God. Resist the devil, and he will flee from you" (James 4:7).

If you don't resist the devil, he won't flee. It's God's power standing behind you making it work, but nonetheless, the devil flees from you. You can't ask God to rebuke the devil for you. He's given that authority to you!

Many Christians today pray and then passively stand, and stand, and stand in "faith" patiently waiting until finally—maybe—they receive their answer. If they do receive, it's because they're like a dog with a bone. Refusing to let go, they stand there through all of the pain, circumstances, and persecution the devil throws at them. They receive their answer by default because they're still standing after Satan's hurled his worst. These believers simply fail (1) to recognize that the devil is hindering their answer from manifesting and (2) to exercise the power and authority they've been given to do something about it.

As a born-again believer, you don't have to pray the way Old Testament people did. For the sake of illustration, let's say Daniel was born again and had the privileges of a New Testament believer there in chapter 10. After praying and not seeing his answer manifest within three minutes, he could have said, "God, You're the same yesterday, today, and forever. (Heb. 13:8.) If You gave the commandment at the beginning of my supplication last time, I know You did the same thing this time. You've already answered. Father, I thank You that it's on its way. Since You've already given the command, would You please tell me what's the holdup?"

And God would've shown Daniel, "There's demonic opposition against your prayer." Then he could've stood up and rebuked that demonic power. As a born-again believer, Daniel could've taken authority over the devil and commanded him to get out of the way. This would have dramatically shortened the period of time between "amen" and "there it is" (manifestation). Daniel could've done that as a New Testament believer. As an Old Testament saint, he couldn't. All he could do was stand.

But if you understand these principles, you'll have great comfort knowing that God has already done it. He has already commanded your answer, but it must come from the spiritual world into the physical world. There are a number of things that can happen to hinder that. I don't have enough space in this book to list everything He's shown me, but I'll give you several examples to help illustrate.

CHAPTER 11

The Answer Is in the Spirit

Many people pray for provision and then expect God to instantly manifest their answer. If it doesn't happen, then they start doubting and say, "God, why haven't You done anything?" No, the Lord has already done His part. He's already commanded financial blessing upon all believers. (Deut. 8:18.) God has already given every Christian power, anointing, and ability to prosper. Psalm 35:27 reveals His delight "in the prosperity of his servant." In the spirit, there's abundant supply for every born-again believer. (2 Cor. 8:9.)

God Himself doesn't give you the money. He gives you power to get wealth, but He doesn't drop the cash in your wallet directly. The Lord gives you an anointing—an ability—and then you must go out and set your hand to something. One of the reasons why many Christians who are praying for financial blessing haven't seen it manifest yet is because they think God gives it to them directly. God will bless the work of your hands, but first you have to do something!

His Provision Comes Through People

You can hinder what God has already commanded and done in the spirit from manifesting in the physical realm. Many people stay on welfare because they can't make as much money at McDonald's. So they do nothing and continue to pray for God to dump provision into their lap. God can't bless and multiply welfare, because you aren't doing anything to get it. But if you'd go out and work at McDonald's—even if you had to take a cut in pay from welfare—God could begin to multiply that. As you work, He can prosper and bring finances to you.

God uses people to bless you.

"Give, and it shall be given unto you; good measure, pressed down, and shaken together, and running over, *shall men give* into your bosom" (Luke 6:38, emphasis mine).

He sends His financial provision to you through people.

Money is an earthly institution. God Himself doesn't use it. Neither will we in heaven. Sure, there are gold, silver, and precious stones in heaven, but they're not used for exchange. Money is a human invention, which we use here on earth.

God isn't going to counterfeit your country's currency and give it to you. Money's not going to just rain out of the sky. I heard a man say one time that if you'd send him ten dollars, he'd mail you a green string. He said that if you put that green string in your wallet, God would use it to create money, and you'd never be broke again. That's a trick! It can't happen. God doesn't do those kinds of things; He uses people.

So when you pray about a financial need, God will use people to help meet that need. It won't just fall out of the sky. If you're looking for your ship to come in, but you've never sent one out, you're going to be disappointed. You'll think, *God, why didn't You answer my prayer?* He did! He's blessed you with all spiritual blessings. He's commanded His favor upon you. He's given you power to get wealth. All of these things are real in the spiritual realm. But you need to cooperate in faith!

Sold!

A friend of mine had his house up for sale "By Owner." He'd put a sign up in his yard but had been unable to sell his house for two years. Only a few people had even bothered to look at it. On top of this, the market wasn't that good at the time. Since houses weren't selling, this really became a matter of concern to him.

He heard me teach this message, and the Lord spoke to him saying, "I moved on someone to buy your house the very first day you put it up for sale, but Satan has been hindering them." It wasn't this man's fault, but demonic opposition had been hindering the manifestation of his answer.

Since my friend didn't know what the situation was, he prayed over it in tongues, believing that God was interceding through him. Two days later, his house sold. While they were going through the closing, the man buying the house told my friend, "The very first day you put that sign in your yard, I told my wife, 'That's our house!' I've been trying for two years now to get my finances together, but I haven't been able to. Then the strangest thing happened. Two days ago, the man who'd been trying to buy my house came over with cash and we closed. It's taken me a day or so to get things together so I could come over here and do this. But here I am!"

God had answered my friend's prayer two years before he saw anything happen. The holdup wasn't the Lord who hadn't moved, but Satan who had hindered through other people. If you don't understand this, you'll pray and ask God to sell your house. Then, if it doesn't sell, you'll say, "Lord, why didn't You answer my prayer?" He did. He answers every prayer. It's already done. God has already talked to the people. He's commanded this blessing upon you, but it's in the spiritual realm. By faith, you must bring it out of the spirit and into the physical realm.

Believe It's Done

If you can understand this, it'll make a difference in the way you receive from God. If the manifestation doesn't come right away when I pray for healing now, I don't say, "God, I don't know why You haven't healed me, or this other person, yet. But we're asking You to move!" I don't start fasting and recruiting other people to bombard heaven with me to plead with God and make Him do it. That whole mindset is unbelief. You didn't believe that you received when you prayed.

"What things so ever ye desire, when ye pray, believe that ye receive them, and ye shall have them" (Mark 11:24).

You must believe you receive the very instant you pray, not when you see it. How can you believe God answered your prayer if you don't feel healed right away? The moment you prayed—BOOM—it's already done in the spirit. Your answer is a reality in the spiritual world.

If it doesn't manifest, don't doubt that God has done what His Word said He did! Believe that you received when you prayed. Then continue to pray, not asking for it again, but taking your authority and using it against any demonic powers hindering your answer from coming to pass. Ask God for revelation if there's something you're supposed to do. If you're praying for finances, you might need to get a job or sow some money. But don't doubt that God moved and already did it!

God has already provided everything you need. It's already in the spiritual world. You just need to believe it's done.

Blind in One Eye

Understanding this principle has revolutionized the way I pray! (For more on how this applies to prayer specifically, I recommend my teaching entitled *A Better Way to Pray*.) Not long after the Lord showed me these truths from Daniel 9 and 10, I held a meeting in Childress, Texas. It was 1977, and I preached a message entitled "What to Do When Your Prayers Seem Unanswered." I talked about how God had already done it, that it's not a matter of our waiting for Him to produce healing, but it's already there in the spiritual world. I discussed how faith reaches over into the spirit realm and brings those things into physical manifestation. Therefore, we can control how quickly healing manifests. Since God has already done it, we can make His healing power manifest.

After preaching this message to about a hundred people, I declared, "Let's demonstrate! Is there anyone here who's sick?" A seventeen-year-old boy came forward who was blind in one eye. I laid hands on him, prayed, rebuked everything I knew to do, and commanded him to see. Then I said, "Cover up your good eye and look through the other. How many fingers do I have up?" I held my hand up in front of his face, but he couldn't see anything—not my hand, not light, nothing! There was zero manifestation. I even had to grab his face and turn it toward my hand because he wasn't even looking in the right direction.

When many of the people saw this, they immediately thought, *Well, this doesn't work.* I could feel and hear the moans and groans of unbelief. So I turned around and addressed the crowd saying, "Look, I believe what I'm teaching is true. We haven't seen it manifest, but it's not because God hasn't healed him. It's not because we're waiting on God to do something. It's because we're having trouble getting it from the spiritual realm into the physical. It's our fault, not God's! You're welcome to leave if you want to. But if you believe what I taught and would like to stay and pray with me, you're welcome to." About twenty-five stayed.

So we gathered around this boy and started praying for him. We weren't asking, "O God, You didn't do it the first time. Please heal him now!" Instead, we were saying, "Father, we believe it's true. You've already healed him. Your power has already been released. We bind whatever it is that's keeping this from coming into physical manifestation. Give us wisdom and show us what's going on." We also prayed in tongues in order to build ourselves up in faith, according to Jude 20.

This continued for about half an hour. Every five minutes or so, I'd stop, have this boy cover up his good eye and look through the other one. He was never able to see my hand. I was really seeking God for wisdom!

Healing or Miracle?

All of a sudden, the Lord said, "He doesn't need a healing; he needs a miracle!" As that impression came to me, my next thought was, *What's the difference?* I'd never considered the difference between the two before. Since then I've understood some, but it's still an area I'm learning about. However, that was the first time I'd ever thought about it. Outwardly, I was praying away in tongues. Inwardly, I was wondering, *Is this really God? What's the difference between a healing and a miracle? Would that somehow affect the way we're praying?*

Then Don Krow—my associate pastor, who's still with me today—spoke up and said, "Andrew, God told me that he doesn't need a healing; he needs a miracle!" It was word for word what the Lord had just spoken to my heart. So we stopped, and I asked this boy, "What's wrong with your eye anyway?"

"When I was a baby, I had an eye infection. They operated on me and surgically removed my lens and retina. I don't even have the necessary parts to be able to see!"

As soon as he said that, I replied, "You don't need a healing; you need a miracle! You need God to give you a creative miracle and put those things in there." So I cupped my hands over his face and declared, "Lens and retina, I command you to come into this eye in Jesus' name!"

Then I had him cover up his good eye and look through the other one. I asked, "How many fingers do I have up?" He answered, "1, 2 ..." and he could see! The Lord had opened his eye!

God had released that power before this boy had ever been born. Through Jesus, it had already been provided and was available in the spirit realm. At the very moment we prayed, God's power was in motion to bring this miracle into physical manifestation. But there were some hindrances.

Stick With It!

I still don't understand everything. I'm not sure why I had to receive a revelation that it wasn't a healing but a miracle. I believe that was for me. When Don confirmed it, my faith quickened and surged. That's when I took authority and spoke to the mountain. (Mark 11:23.) Most people don't speak directly to their problem. Instead, they talk to God about it. The Word says to speak to the mountain!

The problem was this boy didn't have a lens or retina to be able to see. So I had to speak to them.

"Death and life are in the power of the tongue: and they that love it shall eat the fruit thereof" (Prov. 18:21).

When all of this happened, my faith quickened, and I commanded the lens and retina to come into his eye. Then he could see!

If we hadn't persisted in prayer, this boy's eye might have never seen. It wouldn't have been because God didn't do it. He had already made the provision, and it was available in the spirit. But most people, if they don't see the manifestation in a certain amount of time, give in to discouragement, doubt, and unbelief.

We do others a disservice when we pray for their healing but let them go before it's manifest. I have some very good friends with healing ministries who pray down the line for people and never look back. They refuse to even think about it because they don't want to slip into unbelief. This works to a degree. Some good things do happen, but that method is fraught with all kinds of problems because most people's faith—without manifestation over time—becomes weaker, not stronger.

CHAPTER 12

God Has Already Provided

God has already done it. He's already provided. Everything we ever need is already a done deal. As soon as we believe and begin learning how His power works—we can make things manifest!

Many of the greatest healing evangelists understood this concept. They might not have taught it from the same scriptures or expressed it in the same terminology, but they believed it.

John G. Lake had over 100,000 confirmed, documented cases of healing. They actually closed down a hospital in Spokane, Washington, for a period of time because so few people needed their services. He and his "healing technicians" were that effective!

Since Lake had such a fruitful ministry, we ought to consider his opinion. He felt that the main reason why people didn't see healing manifest in their lives was passivity in receiving. They would pray, ask, and then passively wait on God to heal them, not understanding that He'd already done it. Instead of taking their authority and commanding healing into manifestation now, they let it drag out over days, weeks, months, and years. They didn't understand how to believe God and make what He had already done in the spirit come into the physical world. In John G. Lake's estimation, that was the number one problem.

God has already done it. Believe it's already been provided, and then receive it by faith. If you don't immediately see the physical manifestation of what you prayed for, then you need to get in and start battling your own unbelief. Receive wisdom if there's something you need to do. If there's demonic power involved, break it. But the Scripture clearly establishes the principle that God has already done it.

Atmosphere of Unbelief

Jesus operated in this same understanding.

And he [Jesus] cometh to Bethsaida; and they bring a blind man unto him, and besought him to touch him. And he took the blind man by the hand, and led him out of the town; and when he had spit on his eyes, and put his hands upon him, he asked him if he saw ought. And he looked up, and said, I see men as trees, walking. After that he put his hands again upon his eyes, and made him look up: and he was restored, and saw every man clearly. And he sent him away to his house, saying, Neither go into the town, nor tell it to any in the town.

Mark 8:22-26, brackets mine

This is an unusual example of healing. It's the only time in Scripture where Jesus asked a person something like "How is it?" after He prayed for them. It's also the only time He ever prayed for a physical need a second time. So this was a very unique situation.

Notice, first of all, that Jesus was in Bethsaida. He took the blind man by the hand and led him out of the town. Some people think Jesus did weird things just to keep us off balance. They say,

"You can never figure God out. He's got no rhyme or reason. He just delights in doing things in unusual ways!" Not true! This was the Creator of the universe in all its meticulous detail. Everything is perfect and works together in harmony. You can predict where the stars will be a million years from now—should the Lord tarry—or ten thousand years ago because it's so ordered. It's absurd to think that the God of order Himself would do things in a completely random manner. It's simply not true!

Jesus led this man out of the town because Bethsaida was one of the worst places He'd ever been!

"Woe unto thee, Bethsaida! for if the mighty works had been done in Tyre and Sidon, which have been done in you, they had a great while ago repented, sitting in sackcloth and ashes" (Luke 10:13).

Jesus pronounced judgment upon Bethsaida because of all its unbelief. The Lord encountered this in His own hometown of Nazareth too.

"And he could there do no mighty work, save that he laid his hands upon a few sick folk, and healed them. And he marvelled because of their unbelief" (Mark 6:5, 6).

Jesus wanted to do more in those places, but couldn't. These people weren't in faith, so He couldn't pray for them other than for a few minor things.

Jesus operated in faith 100 percent. So we know that there was no problem with Him. But there must be some degree of faith on the part of those receiving. Now, I believe that's been blown way out of proportion. We sometimes use this as an excuse to put all the blame on the person receiving if the healing doesn't manifest. That's too simplistic! More often than not, it's the fault of the person praying as much as it is the person receiving. However, with all that being said, it's still true that there must be some degree of faith operating in the person receiving the healing.

"How Is It?"

Knowing that, Jesus took this blind man by the hand and led him out of the town. The Lord was busy—infinitely more than I am. If you need healing today, I can't come pray for you. I don't have time to take you by the hand and walk you an hour out into the countryside to pray. Jesus wasn't just taking a stroll. His purpose was to get this man away from the unbelief in Bethsaida, knowing that it could hinder God's power from manifesting his healing.

However, even though Jesus got this man out of town, He perceived that He hadn't gotten all of this town out of the man. He discerned that this man was still being affected by that atmosphere of unbelief. So after He prayed for him, He asked, "What do you see?"

Now Jesus wasn't asking, "Did God answer My prayer? Did anything happen?" No, that would've been unbelief. The Word says you must believe you receive when you pray. For Jesus to have asked "Did it work?" would have violated His own teaching. The Lord knew that God had moved. He knew God's power was present, but it was in the spirit realm and needed to come into the physical. Jesus was aware that the unbelief of that town and the effect it had on that man was hindering an instantaneous, full manifestation of what God had already done.

So Jesus asked, "How is it?" The man answered, "I see men as trees, walking" (Mark 8:24). In other words, God's power had manifested to a degree. The man had been totally blind before, but now he could see a little bit. So Jesus did something unusual again. He laid hands on him and prayed a second time.

"But it's unbelief to pray for something twice!" It is if you ask twice. Then at least one of the two times, you prayed in unbelief. You must believe you receive when you pray. However, it's not unbelief to continue to pray, taking your authority and making what He's already provided manifest.

Confront Hindrances Head On!

It's not wrong to continue to pray if you understand that God has already released His power. In the spirit realm, it's complete. But you don't want it to just stay in the spirit. You want it manifest in the physical. So you pray again, not doubting that God has already given, but to rebuke the devil. You pray to receive wisdom and revelation in case there's something you must do. You pray to build up your faith and encourage yourself. Instead of just praying once and then trying to forget it, you're aggressively releasing your faith to deal with any hindrance and draw the provision into the physical realm.

Jesus confronted the hindrances head on. He didn't doubt His Father's faithfulness but doubted this man's faithfulness—that the unbelief of this town was still hindering him from receiving. So He asked the man this question and saw that there was still some delay in the manifestation. Instead of just letting him go, Jesus kept ministering to him until he received the full healing. It's much easier to keep something you've already got than to get something you don't yet have.

So Jesus prayed for the man a second time. If Satan, unbelief, or whatever the hindrance is can withstand one dose of the Holy Ghost, shoot 'em again! Just hit 'em again with the same power. This time, those eyes received, and he saw every man clearly.

Then Jesus told him not to go into the town or tell it to anyone there. He instructed the man to go home, but where do you think he lived? This man may have had a job, family, and friends. Yet Jesus commanded him not to tell anybody or to go back into Bethsaida. That's a pretty strict requirement! Why? Jesus knew that even though this man had received the manifestation of healing, he could still lose it if he immediately got back around all of that unbelief.

Retention of your healing isn't automatically guaranteed. Jesus warned the man who'd been healed at the pool of Bethesda, "Sin no more, lest a worse thing come unto thee" (John 5:14). The devil comes "to steal, and to kill, and to destroy" (John 10:10). There's nothing he'd like better than to take away your manifestation, kill your faith, and destroy your testimony. You must maintain your healing by faith. That's why Jesus told the man not to go back into that unbelieving situation.

Jesus knew that God had healed this man completely. It was already done. But He recognized that there was a hindrance in getting it from the spiritual into the physical. So the Lord prayed with him a second time in order to get this man over that hindrance. Then He told him how to keep the healing he'd received.

I often encounter this same thing. People come to my meetings, and we help them manifest a healing. Then they go back into unbelieving churches and submit themselves to a teaching which is totally opposite what they receive from me. Their sickness or disease returns, and then they come back to me the next time I'm in town and ask, "What's happened?" It's not God who took the healing away or put sickness back on them. They quit believing. They didn't have any root in themselves and so only endured for a season. (Mark 4:17.)

Cooperate & Command

God has already done everything. You're already blessed, healed, and prosperous. You already have joy, peace, and wisdom. Everything you could ever need is already there—in the spirit. All you need to do is believe and receive!

If you don't see the manifestation immediately, don't doubt that God has already done it. Recognize that He's a Spirit and that He moves in the spirit realm. (John 4:24.) For what He's done—what's already true in the spirit—to manifest in the physical realm requires the cooperation of some physical human being. Faith is the bridge that God's provision crosses over, out of the spirit and into the physical. Sometimes it takes us a period of time to build ourselves up in faith to the point where we can receive, but it doesn't take God any time to be ready to give, because He's already provided.

Sometimes it's demonic opposition that hinders what God has already done from coming into manifestation. Sometimes other people are involved in our answers to prayer. Therefore, we must receive wisdom about how Satan is hindering so we can speak to the mountain and command it to be removed.

We need to learn and cooperate with the laws of God. You resist the devil. You speak directly to the problem. You exercise the authority and power God has given you. It's important to direct your prayers properly in order to receive your desired results. God has already done it, but it's your responsibility to believe and draw His provision into the natural realm. As soon as you can get yourself into faith and learn how to do this, you can manifest what God has already done.

Instead of being a beggar, a pleader, a whiner, and a griper, you'll become a commander. You'll believe what God has said He's done, and you'll take your authority and begin commanding it to manifest. Instead of just praying for healing, you'll command healing. Instead of just praying for blessing, you'll command blessing. That's a huge difference!

Be a Bridge!

You need to understand that there's a real spiritual world. Through the window of God's Word, you can see and accurately perceive the spirit realm. As you discover and meditate on what other people did and what was going on behind the scenes, you can be confident that the same thing is going on around you today. Even though you can't see it or feel it with your physical senses, you can perceive it with the eyes of your heart.

Renew your mind to God's Word, and allow yourself to become a bridge that He can flow through from the spiritual realm into this physical world!

CHAPTER 13

The Battlefield

God is a Spirit, and He moves in the spiritual world. (John 4:24.) Everything God has provided—by grace—is already a reality in the spiritual realm. But whether or not they ever manifest themselves in the physical realm depends on our ability to receive—not God's giving.

There are things we can do to shorten the manifestation time. There are also things we can do to delay it. Dealing with the devil and overcoming his hindrances to the manifestation of what God has already provided is popularly called "spiritual warfare." Since there has been such a large emphasis on this in recent times, these next few chapters may possibly be the most controversial of this entire book.

Spiritual Warfare

Satan does exist. There is evil in this world. Demonic forces are fighting against God and His kingdom. Prior to the last couple of decades, most of the Body of Christ had been very ignorant of Satan's devices. Many believed that all the devils were over in Africa or some other undeveloped part of the world. But they didn't believe that any of the western, developed, "civilized" countries had any such thing as demonic activity. In the past twenty-plus years, that notion has been thoroughly shattered, especially among charismatic Christians. There still may be some evangelicals and mainline denominational folks who are unaware, but not very many.

Anyone who truly believes the Word of God has to acknowledge that Satan is a real foe. The devil tempted Jesus and opposed Him during His entire ministry. The Bible records many instances where the Lord healed people by casting out demons.

"God anointed Jesus of Nazareth with the Holy Ghost and with power: who went about doing good, and healing all that were oppressed of the devil; for God was with him" (Acts 10:38).

God's Word is very clear that sickness and disease are oppressions from the devil.

Overall, it's been good for Christians to recognize the fact that Satan exists and his demonic powers are active today. However, in the process, much of the Body of Christ has swung from ignorance to a very weird extreme. That's why many "spiritual warfare" teachings and practices today actually credit the devil with abilities and powers he doesn't really have.

Satan is a factor. He does hinder what God has already done in the spiritual realm from manifesting in the physical realm. It is important to learn how to resist the devil and take authority over him. But I want to make it crystal clear that Satan is a defeated foe! The only reason he's able to do anything is because of our own ignorance, unbelief, and fear. Although the Body of Christ today has come to an awareness of the devil's existence, they have remained, for the most part, functionally ignorant of Satan's true devices. (2 Cor. 2:11.)

Between Your Ears

Again, the book of Ephesians was written from the standpoint that everything has already been done. It's just a matter now of possessing what God has already provided, not trying to get Him to give us something new. With this in mind, let's look at how Paul winds this letter down in the last chapter.

Finally, my brethren, be strong in the Lord, and in the power of his might. Put on the whole armour of God, that ye may be able to stand against the wiles of the devil. For we wrestle not against flesh and blood, but against principalities, against powers, against the rulers of the darkness of this world, against spiritual wickedness in high places.

Ephesians 6:10-12

These verses make it very clear that we're in a battle—and those who don't believe it are destined to lose!

However, the battle is between your ears! It's not out there somewhere in the "heavenly places." It's in your mind.

Now, before you take offense, I encourage you to go ahead and fully read what I'm saying. See the scriptures for yourself, and then draw your conclusions from the Word, not just current teaching and popular examples being promoted in the Body of Christ today.

We are in a battle, but it's not out there in the heavenly places. We are fighting demonic powers—and they do exist in heavenly places—but the battlefield (place of engagement) is your mind.

Deception & Lies

Notice verse 11:

"Put on the whole armour of God, that ye may be able to stand against the wiles of the devil."

Wiles are lies, cunningness, and craftinesss. All of these words imply that Satan's only power is deception. He doesn't have actual power of his own to force anyone to do anything. We must surrender ourselves to him first. Therefore, the devil is really a non-factor to those who know and understand the truth.

I'll be establishing this in many other scriptures, but allow me to make some additional statements first. Again, I challenge you to follow through until I get to the verses that verify these things. Don't just set this book aside because it's contrary to "popular theology" today. As a believer in Christ, you need to understand the truth!

Satan is an absolutely defeated foe! He has zero power to do anything. All he can do is deceive you through wiles, cunningness, craftiness, and lies, and then use the very power you surrender to him against you. That's why ignorance is so expensive! The devil's goal is to keep you ignorant of the truth and believing his lies.

After soundly rebuking the Corinthians for falling into all kinds of weird things, Paul confided:

"I fear, lest by any means, as the serpent *beguiled* Eve through his *subtilty,* so your minds should be *corrupted* from the simplicity that is in Christ" (2 Cor. 11:3, emphasis mine).

Notice all the words denoting deceptive practices: "beguiled," "subtlety," and "corrupted." Satan comes against us by corrupting our minds from the simplicity that's in Christ. In other words, he tries to make us think that the Gospel is harder than it really is.

Tempted

In Genesis, why didn't the devil choose a tiger? He could have intimidated Eve with a roar or two. Why didn't he have a wooly mammoth just stick its foot on top of her head and demand, "Eat this fruit or I'll crush your skull"? Why did Satan choose the serpent—the craftiest animal on the face of the earth—to come against Eve? Because the devil knew he had absolutely no power to force or intimidate Adam or Eve into anything. He had to deceive them instead! (Gen. 3:1.)

Satan started the deception by asking, "Has God really said…?" (Gen. 3:1). He challenged the Word of God. It's the truth of God's Word that enables us to seek God, yield to Him, and resist the devil. If Satan hadn't challenged the Word and gotten them to question and second-guess it, his temptation would've gone nowhere. The serpent didn't come to force or intimidate, but to deceive. (My teaching entitled *Christian Philosophy* goes into much more detail on this subject. It's basically an in-depth study of Genesis 3.)

Satan tempted Adam and Eve with something they already had. He asked, "Don't you want to be like God?" The truth was, they were already like Him. In fact, they were more like God before they ate of the fruit of the Tree of the Knowledge of Good and Evil than they were afterwards.

The devil says, "Oh sure, God loves the world. But what makes you think He loves you?" Then he gets you into feeling and trying in some physical, natural way to discern whether or not God loves you. There you are on the devil's turf in the physical realm not understanding from God's Word that in the spiritual realm, it's already done. Because you don't feel loved, and you don't have any goose bumps, you pray, "O God, please pour out Your love in my life," which is actually a prayer of unbelief!

Satan loves to hinder people from coming to the Lord, but his only "power" is deception and lies. The devil can't keep you from doing anything. If he could, he would have kept you from being born again. You were at your worst and your weakest. You hadn't been going to church, fasting, praying, studying the Word, tithing, or living right. You might even have been an adulterer, a dope addict, mean, selfish, etc. Yet in that dismal state, you called out and received the greatest miracle of all—the new birth. If Satan were really as powerful as he claims to be, then he would have kept you from receiving salvation. Instead, all he can do is taunt you immediately afterwards, saying, "You didn't get it, you didn't get it!" He can't stop you from doing anything! Satan can't do anything to you without your consent and cooperation.

The devil would rather you not be born again, but now that you're saved, the next best thing is to persuade you to say, "Oh sure, God can do these things, but He hasn't done them yet." Satan loves that!

Don't Fall on Your Can!

I remember playing tug-of-war as a kid. There'd be two teams pulling on opposite ends of a long rope over a large mud hole. As a boy, my team and I tried our best to pull the other side into the mud. However, if we saw them winning—and that mud pit drawing nearer—we'd just let go of the rope. We might not have won, but at least the other team fell on their cans doing it!

Satan does the same thing today. If he can't prevent you from winning, he'll shift gears to catch you off guard and make you fall down on your can! Basically, he comes to believers and says, "If you're really such a great Christian, why don't you have this and do that?" The devil will condemn you over what you don't have and try to keep you focused on just the physical realm.

But the truth is, in the spirit, you already have everything. The key to seeing what you have in the spirit manifest in your life is believing and acknowledging it.

"That the communication of thy faith may become effectual by the acknowledging of every good thing which is in you in Christ Jesus" (Philem. 1:6).

The way you get your faith to work is by starting to acknowledge the good things in you in Christ!

However, most Christians say, "There isn't any good thing in me!" and point to Romans 7.

"For I know that in me (*that is, in my flesh,*) dwelleth no good thing" (Rom. 7:18, emphasis mine).

You need to understand the parentheses to properly interpret this verse. This wouldn't have been a true statement had Paul left out "that is, in my flesh," because in him dwelt God Himself—and everything God is and had given him—which is good. But Paul specified his flesh—his physical, carnal, natural, not born-again self. It's fine for a Christian to understand that in their flesh—apart from Christ—they are nothing. But in Christ, they can do all things and much good dwells within. To live in victory, you need to be focused on who you are in Christ!

Satan aims his warfare here. He specifically targets your understanding and acknowledging of who you are and what you have in Christ. All he has are lies and deception. The devil doesn't have any more power to make you fail in any area of your life than he had to make Adam and Eve fail. He has to deceive you.

Complete in Christ

If you were the devil trying to deceive Adam and Eve, how would you do it? They'd never sinned, never had any kind of problems, and lived in paradise with plenty of food. Basically, they were perfect people living perfect lives in a perfect place. How do you tempt someone like that?

He couldn't tempt them with money—there wasn't such a thing. Every need was abundantly supplied. He couldn't tempt them with adultery; there wasn't anyone else to commit adultery with. He couldn't tempt them with hurt, pain, and bitterness over past experiences; there was nothing in them that depression or discouragement could latch on to. Perfect people living in a perfect place couldn't be tempted by money, sex, power, glory, etc. What could they be tempted with?

Satan lied to them by saying, "You don't have it all. As good as this is, there's more!" The truth is, they did have it all. But the devil enticed them to speculate about what might be, what could be. Through that, he caused perfect people living perfect lives in a perfect place to fall.

Adam and Eve threw it all away because a talking snake convinced them that they didn't have enough. Most people today would give anything to live in such a perfect situation. If you could convince perfect people living in paradise with no physical problems whatsoever to think they didn't have it all, to doubt God's Word, and to question His goodness, then I guarantee you can convince people living in a fallen world who can look in any direction and see pain, tragedy, lack, and need that they don't have it all.

But the truth is, if you've been born again, you do have everything. You are complete in Christ. (Col. 2:10.) Everything you'll ever need has already been given to you. You're not standing and fighting against some demonic entity with superior power and authority. Instead, all you're doing is combating his lies and deceptions—the same ones he used on Adam and Eve. (My teaching *The Believer's Authority* goes into much more detail on this.)

Processes of Your Mind

The battle against the devil is waged in your thoughts. That's why God's Word is so essential! Satan's only power is deception.

He lies and represents himself as more powerful than he is. But truth is the antidote to deception.

"And ye shall know the truth, and the truth shall make you free" (John 8:32).

If you know the truth, the truth will set you free.

*For though we walk in the flesh, we do not war after the flesh: (For the weapons of our warfare are not carnal, but mighty through God to the pulling down of **strong holds;**) Casting down **imaginations,** and every high thing that exalteth itself against the **knowledge** of God, and bringing into captivity every **thought** to the obedience of Christ.*

2 Corinthians 10:3-5, emphasis mine

Notice how our warfare is against thoughts, imaginations, strongholds, and knowledge that comes against the Word of God. These are all processes of your mind.

Satan is powerless unless you believe his lies and fall into his deception. Most Christians believe the devil has tremendous power and authority, much more than we do as physical human beings. That's simply not true. Satan is a defeated foe. Although he's been beaten, he walks about "as a roaring lion...seeking whom he may devour" (1 Peter 5:8). The devil isn't a true lion; he just walks around roaring like one trying to intimidate the Body of Christ. But the truth is, he's had his teeth pulled, and all he can do now is gum you. Apart from the power you give him through believing his lies, Satan can't steal anything from you. He uses ignorance, fear, and unbelief to oppress and destroy.

CHAPTER 14

───────

Delivered!

The devil is a factor, but not because he's superior in power and authority. He deceives people, and they yield to him through fear. This is what actually empowers him. Satan takes a person's own fear and uses it against them to eat their lunch and pop the bag!

My awareness of the spiritual realm increased dramatically in 1968 when I first became really turned on to the Lord. I not only realized that God was alive and well but also that many things happening in this world were caused by demons. The denomination I was raised in believed that all the devils were over in Africa. They didn't think there were such things as "demons" here in America. It was a non-issue. It wasn't even practical to talk about it! But as I started reading the Word, this truth just jumped out at me. The Holy Spirit showed me that many problems—especially sickness, disease, and emotional problems—were demonic in origin. So I started praying for people and seeing them delivered!

We didn't know very much, but God did some awesome things. We saw addicts come off of drugs instantly with no withdrawal. We also saw homosexuals completely set free. Although we experienced some great successes, we were still quite ignorant of Satan's devices. We knew there was warfare, but we didn't know exactly how it worked. It was as if we were fighting the devil with our eyes closed, just flailing in the air. Then, every once in a while, we'd actually hit him and see some awesome victories.

Mistakes

But there were some bad things that came out of this too. I read a book on deliverance by a fellow who focused almost exclusively on this aspect of ministry. I mentioned his name once in a meeting, and a lady came up to me afterwards who had been a member of his church for several years. She told me that while she attended there, the devil just destroyed both her and her family. Based on her personal knowledge of how this man and his ministry were plagued by demonic powers, she encouraged me that what I was sharing from the Word about Satan is true.

We read this man's book out of sheer desperation, trying to figure out deliverance. He taught that you had to see some physical manifestation—like vomiting—whenever someone got delivered. You also had to talk to the demons and ask them their names. Then, once you found out the "strongman," you had to cast them into a certain place. You couldn't just cast them out; you had to tell them where to go! He also said that you couldn't do it by yourself; there always had to be at least two people present to minister because the demons could overcome just one, and there were all these other things that really had no scriptural precedent. They were just this man's personal example. I'm not saying he's of the devil, just that he made some mistakes.

I've made some mistakes ministering deliverance too! Many of them were based on the information we received from reading this book. We used to counsel people for three weeks in order to "prep" them for deliverance. Some people still require that today! I know someone here in Colorado Springs who went for deliverance and had to fill out a five-page form. He had to make an appointment and wait forty-five days in order to go and be set free of demons. That's absolutely foolish! Jesus never made people fill out any forms. Neither did He require them to wait for ministry a whole month and a half. I'm not condemning anyone, because I used to do it that way too. However, since then I've found better ways to cast out demons.

Spaced Out!

My friends and I were fringe Baptists when I saw my first demonic manifestation and knew for sure what it was. As Baptists, we were pretty radical due to our belief in supernatural things like demonization and speaking in tongues. A certain woman had come to our little Baptist church and received the Lord. Although soundly converted, she still had some problems she was working through as a former lesbian.

One day at work, she just completely flipped out. She didn't know her name, where she'd come from, or even what she was doing in that building. Literally losing her mind, she didn't know anything. Someone walked up to her, called her by name, and said, "I'll meet you after work, and you can ride home with me." From that person, she figured out her name. After following the woman home, she looked in her purse, found some keys, and one of them opened the door. That's where we found her—at home and totally spaced out!

We believed this was demonic. If we'd have taken her to some government agency, they would've put her in a mental ward somewhere, doped her up, and she probably never would've been the same again. Therefore, we knew the answer was spiritual, not physical.

We just took her and locked her in a room. We didn't know anything, other than this was obviously the devil. So we just started praying and singing songs. That's when this woman became violent. One time, when we were holding her down, she—with one arm—took two of us and threw us over her head and against a wall. Now that's supernatural strength, just like Legion in the Bible! (Luke 8:29-30.)

So we began seeing demonic manifestations. We just locked her in that room and took shifts with her, refusing to give up. Even though we didn't know exactly how to minister deliverance to her, over seven days we saw all kinds of demons come out through our persistence and faith. Because of that, fame spread and people came. We saw many set free, but we also fell into some of this weirdness (i.e., empowering the devil and giving him much more credit than is due).

"Not Tonight!"

One Wednesday evening, a homosexual man we'd been dealing with several weeks in preparation for deliverance came to the mid-week service. He'd brought with him another homosexual who needed to be delivered too. He told me, "I'm ready to be delivered tonight!"

I answered, "Not tonight."

"Why not?"

"Because it's just me by myself. The associate pastor is gone to a conference." We were the ones casting demons out of people.

He answered, "I'm not leaving this place with these demons!"

"And I'm not casting them out!"

He looked right at me and declared, "You'd better do something, because I'm not leaving with them."

I had no idea what to do, so I got Jamie. She wasn't my wife yet, but we were prayer partners. She'd never seen a demon cast out of someone before. In fact, she wasn't even baptized in the Holy Spirit yet! But Jamie went with me into the back room of that church.

This room had windows on two sides and chairs stacked on top of each other all along the wall. I started talking to this guy and saying, "I'm not doing this."

He answered, "You'd better plead the blood!" That's another weird concept we were taught. We had to "plead the blood" to keep the demons from coming out of them and entering us. It's totally inaccurate!

I started praying, "Father, I don't know what to do!" Immediately, this guy fell to the ground, started barking like a dog, writhing like a snake, and throwing chairs up against the windows. The other demonized fellow climbed up on top of a stack of ten chairs. Jamie stood there praying as fast and furious as she could!

Super Simple

I didn't know what to do, so I started asking the demons their names. "What's your name? In the name of Jesus, tell me your name!" Without going into all of the details, we had elaborate systems for naming and talking to them. All kinds of demonic manifestations happened.

These demons were making a fool of me. They'd manifest, name themselves, and leave before another started manifesting. In desperation, I prayed, "O God, help me!" The Lord simply reminded me of where He'd commanded the evil spirits to shut up and come out. (Mark 1:25.) I thought, *Well, that'd be good.* So I declared "In the name of Jesus, I command all of you to shut up and come out of this man!" and—BOOM—he instantly stopped.

This guy fell to the floor and appeared to be dead. But when I rolled him over, he was worshiping God, saying, "Thank You, Jesus! I'm free! They're gone. Thank You!" He'd been totally set free. We suspect that at least ten demons left this man.

I thought to myself, *That was super simple compared to what we normally do!* We had grown accustomed to talking to them, asking their names, and doing all this other stuff. I just resolved right then, "I've been giving the devil too much place." I'd been thinking I had to plead the blood, have at least two people present, etc., etc., etc. But it wasn't any of that stuff! I just spoke in faith and—

BOOM—they were gone. As I studied the Word, my boldness grew as I discovered that this was how Jesus did it.

Physically Attacked

During that period of time, I inadvertently put too much of my focus on the devil. Since there were so many people coming to us for deliverance and so much demonic stuff happening, we were constantly talking about Satan. I found myself spending more time speaking to the devil in "prayer" than God (back then I'd pray two to four hours a day). I knew something had to be wrong with that.

Many people today are into this weird type of "spiritual warfare." Their whole "prayer life" is wrapped up in binding and rebuking the devil. In the process, they're constantly addressing and talking to Satan during their prayer time more than they talk to God. Something's wrong with that!

During this same time, I was trying to open Arlington Christian Center in Arlington, Texas. We rented a building that had previously been a fraternity house. We were going to turn this facility into a place where we could house and minister to people with demonic problems. We painted it and were in the process of cleaning it out.

One evening, I led an all-night prayer meeting there with my church. Everyone else had already come, prayed, and gone, so I was left in that building by myself. As I continued to pray, something in that room began to choke me. I didn't see anything, but I was physically being choked and beaten. Demons physically attacked me!

"What Do You Mean?"

I ran out of that building, locked the door behind me, and jumped in my car. After backing out of the driveway, I was just about to peel rubber and hightail it out of there when the Lord spoke to me. He asked, "Where are you going?"

I responded, "God, I'm getting out of here. There are demons in that building!"

He calmly continued, "In Ephesians 6, all of the armor you use against the devil is for the front. There's no armor for the back."

Although I asked Him, "What do You mean?" I already knew in my heart. He meant that I couldn't turn my back on the devil. I had to face him. But I went ahead and asked Him again anyway, saying, "Lord, what do You mean? You wouldn't want me to go back in that house, would You?" Silence.

The Lord won't argue with you. He'll just make a statement and let you decide what you're going to do with it. This was about two or three o'clock in the morning. After sitting in that car for a while, I finally pulled back into the driveway, turned the engine off, and went back in. I locked myself in that house and fought those demonic powers until six in the morning. Afterwards, the house was clear, and the demons were gone!

During that time, I also had a number of dreams where Satan would physically attack me. After waking up and thinking, *It's only a dream,* I'd go to the bathroom and find myself bleeding. I definitely experienced some demonic manifestations!

Too Much Credit!

Some people would say, "That's because the devil is powerful, and you were messing with his territory." No, I was giving Satan too much importance in my life with all the time I spent binding and rebuking, learning about, and focusing my attention on him. The Lord showed me that I had glorified the devil and given him more power than he actually had. I immediately repented and decided that the best defense is a good offense. So I started being constant and bold in praising and worshiping God. I believed that if I kept my focus on the Lord, it would totally destroy Satan's inroad into my life.

It's now over thirty years later, and I've never had another demonic manifestation like that. I've had devils manifest around me in people, like when I'm casting them out of someone. (I even have some taped. You can hear the non-human voices and screams coming out of folks.) But I've never had to physically fight a demon since. The only reason it happened then was because I had empowered the devil through my own fear and the undue emphasis I was placing upon him in my life.

This happens over and over again in the Body of Christ today. We've given Satan too much credit. He is a factor, going around seeking whom he may devour, but the only reason the devil can actually do something to someone is because they empower him through their fear. Much of what is being taught as "spiritual warfare" today is ascribing to the devil more power and authority than he really has.

"Spiritual warfare" conferences that ascribe to the devil great power and talk about having to bind ruling principalities over places before anything positive can happen are presenting ideas that are contrary to God's Word. Satan has zero power and zero authority. All he has is deception. But these false concepts are actually causing many Christians to yield to and empower the devil!

CHAPTER 15

The Triumphant Procession

And you, being dead in your sins and the uncircumcision of your flesh, hath he quickened together with him, having forgiven you all trespasses; Blotting out the handwriting of ordinances that was against us, which was contrary to us, and took it out of the way, nailing it to his cross; **And having spoiled principalities and powers, he made a shew of them openly, triumphing over them in it.**

Colossians 2:13-15, emphasis mine

Spoil means "to take everything of value from a conquered foe." It's not talking about fruit and meat that spoils and turns rotten. This kind of "spoil" is from the venue of conquest. It's conquering an enemy and taking everything from them.

Satan, principalities, and all other demonic powers have been spoiled. Through the Cross and Resurrection, Jesus Christ stripped the devil of all power and authority. The first Adam may have surrendered it at the Fall, but the last Adam took it back at the Resurrection. Now Satan has no power or authority. His only weapon is deception. If you yield to the devil's lies, he'll use your power and authority against you!

Show is the same Greek word we get "exhibition" and "exhibit" from. In other words, God exhibited—made an exhibition out of—Satan.

In high school biology, you probably had to catch insects and other things. You'd kill them, mount them, and then write what they were underneath. There they were, impaled by a pin that held them to a piece of poster board. You called it an "exhibit."

That's how I see the devil: impaled, nailed to the cross with the very same spikes that once held Jesus! He's an exhibit—completely stripped of anything of value. Jesus Christ has made a show—an exhibition—of Satan!

The Victory Parade

The phrase translated "triumphing over them" literally refers to the triumphant procession (Col. 2:15). The Romans had a custom of parading the spoils of war and the conquered foe in front of the people after coming home from a conquest. When they went out to fight an enemy, if they conquered, they'd return and have this glorious victory parade. If they didn't win, they wouldn't have this "triumphant procession."

The Roman citizens knew that if they didn't have this parade, the enemy who had been terrorizing them wasn't yet defeated. They'd still be anxious and worry about his return. Their side might have won a great battle, but if they hadn't completely conquered the opposing general or king and had this parade, then the Roman populace would live under constant fear that he might once again marshal his forces against them.

But when they conquered the enemy, the Romans would take this opposing general or king and parade him—dead or alive—to the people. If he was dead, they'd show his severed head and lifeless body. However, they usually preferred to capture him alive. They'd totally strip him of all armor, kingly garments, and jewelry that made him appear strong and important. Completely naked and humiliated, they'd tie him to a horse or chariot. He'd either walk or be dragged through the streets. They'd also cut off both thumbs and big toes so he'd never again be able to hold a sword or stand in battle. In this manner, the Romans paraded their conquered foes.

This triumphant procession showed all the Roman citizens that their enemy had been vanquished. It totally defused all fear that this guy might ever be able to mount another campaign against them. The parade displayed him in such a way that the common people would mock him, beat him, and spit upon him. The purpose of the parade was to completely remove their fear.

The Scripture plainly declares that this is what Jesus did to the devil. He absolutely defeated him at every turn. Christ destroyed "him that had the power of death, that is, the devil" so that He could "deliver them who through fear of death were all their lifetime subject to bondage" (Heb. 2:14, 15). Notice that it's the fear of death that opens the door to bondage. Satan has no power of his own now. He can only come against you with deception. But Jesus has delivered us.

Have You Missed It?

There's been a victory parade—a triumphant procession! The devil has been paraded through the Scriptures and shown to be an absolute zero with the rim knocked off. He's a nothing!

The problem is that most of the Body of Christ has missed the parade—especially among the "spiritual warfare" people. Satan is alive and there is a battle being waged, but it's not in the heavenlies with demonic beings who have awesome power and great authority. All the devil has is his tremendous ability to lie and deceive. Don't glorify Satan! Don't ascribe to him power he doesn't really have! Stand against his lies and believe the truth. Focus your attention on God, not demons. The true battle is in your head. Therefore, remember the parade!

Many "spiritual warfare" people think that you must do all these things before you can go into an area and effectively preach the Gospel. You have to do "spiritual mapping" and discover what ungodly things have happened in the past to create "spiritual strongholds." Then you must send in "intercessors" that spend months, years, and decades praying, rebuking, and binding demonic powers so that the Word of God can finally have an impact. Wrong, wrong, wrong!

There is zero precedent for this in the Word of God! You can't find it anywhere in the New Testament. It's absolutely wrong!

Yes, there are demonic powers. Yes, there is a hierarchy of demons. Yes, they are assigned to specific places. But, NO, that's not how you deal with them! It's a wrong application to preach that the reason more people aren't being born again and set free is because we haven't prayed and done enough "spiritual warfare."

Jesus never sent anyone in advance to pray, bind the devil, and prepare a place so that the Word of God could go forth. He did send His disciples ahead to let people know He was coming. They also did miracles and drew folks to hear Him. But neither Jesus, Peter, nor Paul ever sent believers ahead of them just to pray and do these other things. It's absolutely wrong. (I deal more completely with this in my teaching entitled *A Better Way to Pray*.)

Old Testament vs. the New

In the Old Testament, you'll find different examples of individuals praying for certain cities and specific people. Abraham interceded for the cities of Sodom and Gomorrah. (Gen. 18.) Moses interceded for his siblings and the children of Israel. (Num. 12, 14.) They pleaded for mercy with an angry God who wanted to execute judgment for sin. However, that's very different from today. (These things are also addressed in both *Spiritual Authority* and *The Believer's Authority*.)

There's a huge difference between what happened in the Old Testament and what happens now in the New. In the Old Covenant, Jesus had not yet made atonement for our sins. He hadn't yet gone to hell for us and become our Eternal Intercessor. (Heb. 7:25.) Therefore, it was appropriate for these Old Testament saints to ask for mercy, because mercy wasn't yet totally given. It was being shown in measure, but like it was on credit and not the actual transaction. The atonement had not yet been made.

But on this side of the Cross, there's a huge difference in the way we relate to God. God is pouring out mercy and grace today, not wrath. (2 Cor. 5:19.) He's not imputing men's sins unto them. It's absolutely wrong to think that God is angry at us because of sin and that He's ready to judge this nation. It's incorrect to believe that God is about to unleash judgment unless we repent and the intercessors unite to beg and plead with Him to stay His wrath. Jesus Christ already atoned for all sin. He is the Intercessor to end all of that kind of intercession!

There is a godly type of intercession today. It's simply saying, "Father, I know that You're a good God. You love us. You would've spared Sodom and Gomorrah if there would have only been ten righteous people. There are more than ten righteous people in this country. I know that all of these so-called 'prophecies' saying that unless we repent You're going to send doom, gloom, and destruction aren't from You. Thank You, Father, that You don't want to judge us."

Don't misunderstand me—there are consequences for sin. When people hate God and quit seeking Him, they become mean and selfish. Crime and problems escalate. Tragedies and terrorist attacks happen, but that's just sowing and reaping. Sowing bad seeds and reaping a negative harvest is different than God sending His wrath. God's not bringing judgment on people in this day and age. A time is coming when He will, and He'll be just in doing so. But during the Church Age, He's releasing mercy and grace.

New Testament Intercession

A New Testament intercessor recognizes that God has turned from His wrath because of the atoning work of Jesus Christ.

There's now no need to beg Him for mercy the way Moses did. (Ex. 32:12.) Jesus atoned not only for our sins but for the sins of the entire world. God has turned from His wrath and is now extending mercy and grace to all people everywhere.

It's wrong for a born-again believer to stand there and tell God to repent like Moses did. Moses wasn't wrong, because at the time God was pouring out His wrath. However, we're living in a New Covenant.

"God was in Christ, reconciling the world unto himself, not imputing their trespasses unto them" (2 Cor. 5:19).

To pray, "O God, turn from Your fierce wrath. O God, pour out Your power. Please, move," is to deny the atonement and intercession of the Lord Jesus Christ.

There's a huge difference between the way intercession was done in the Old Testament and the way it's done in the New. Much of what's being taught today as "intercession" and "spiritual warfare" is absolutely an Old Testament mentality. It's anti-Christ. It's denying the truth that Jesus spoiled the devil of all power and authority. It's glorifying Satan. Basically, it's just people who missed the parade!

The Antidote for Deception

True spiritual warfare is fought on a personal level. You resist the lies and deception of the devil. This is primarily done through knowing the truth.

"And ye shall know the truth, and the truth shall make you free" (John 8:32).

Understanding the truth is the antidote for deception.

Deception's power and strength comes from the fact that you don't know you're deceived. But once you realize the proper standard—the truth—deception immediately loses its power.

If someone was terrorizing and threatening to kill you, you'd be afraid. However, if I showed you that person's corpse, your fear would immediately leave. Once you knew the truth of their demise, their threats would no longer intimidate you.

God's Word is truth. (John 17:17.) I take God's Word and meditate on it. Through the Word, I love God and commune with Him. I also fellowship with the Lord's people and stay positive by constantly seeking Him. These are just some practical ways I personally wage spiritual warfare. The best defense is a good offense!

Praise is a very powerful weapon against the devil! It literally drives him out. He can't stand to be around the praise and worship of God. Once every couple of months, I'll rebuke and bind the devil over something, but it's not because he has this awesome power coming against me. It's just that the battle in my mind—my thoughts—has become so intense that I verbalize my resistance, saying, "I rebuke these thoughts in Jesus' name. Satan, you have zero right and zero power over me!" But most of the time, I don't ever have to say anything out loud. I just counter the lies that come my way with truth and continue in constant praise.

This might not be aggressive enough at first if you've been dominated by the devil for a long time. If you're demonized and are trying to come out of it, you might need to emphasize, rebuke, and speak things aloud more. However, once you're free, it's fairly easy to keep that freedom just by staying in the truth.

Send in the Truth!

I used to just rebuke demons in other people when they came to me. But I've come to realize that if I cast a demon out of someone on my faith alone, I'm actually doing them a disservice. (Matt. 12:43-45.) Those evil spirits will just come back on them again if they don't know, understand, and apply the truth against the lies they once believed.

The best way to deliver someone is to tell them the truth. Instruct them in the Word of God. Teach them about the triumphant procession and their victory in Jesus. Help them understand God's promises concerning their problem, and encourage them to diligently apply this truth to their thoughts. I could give you hundreds of testimonies of people who heard me preach the truth of God's Word and were set free from demons without my even so much as rebuking a devil. I'm talking about severe demonizations—people who were non-functional or even doped up and in a mental ward—being completely delivered because they simply listened to the truth and received it in their hearts. They were set free without my even praying for them!

There are other times when I do cast demons out of people. Sometimes Satan has ingrained certain lies so deeply into someone's thinking that they still need another person to pray and rebuke it even though they've seen and embraced the truth. That's why I often cast demons out of people when praying over sickness, depression, and the like. The demons leave and the people get free. But I always impart some truth to them to use for their protection and to keep the devil from coming back in again.

I wage spiritual warfare over a city or a country by sending in the truth! I do that by sharing God's Word through television, radio, tapes, CDs, books, videos, and the Internet. As people hear the truth, their hearts open and become more receptive to the Gospel. Then, I also go in—or send others who have been trained—to preach and teach the Word in person. True spiritual warfare is bringing the truth of God's Word to people!

CHAPTER 16

Proclaim the Word!

Paul is a great example of true spiritual warfare. In Acts 19, the apostle ministered in the city of Ephesus. While there, he experienced much opposition. In fact, Paul considered leaving town, but the Lord told him to stay and build up the believers. Later in Church history, Ephesus became one of the most active and important centers of Christianity. However, despite fierce opposition, Scripture never records Paul ever leading the believers to gather together to intercede, do spiritual warfare, and rebuke the demonic principalities over the city.

At the time, Ephesus was known for the pagan goddess "Diana of the Ephesians." Her majestic and ornate temple was considered one of the wonders of the world. Legend said that her image fell directly from heaven into this temple. That's why devotees from throughout all of Asia came to Ephesus to worship.

Yet Paul never organized the believers to rebuke Diana of the Ephesians. He never invoked them to do "spiritual warfare" against her. What did he do instead? Paul preached the truth. He countered their wrong conceptions and taught the people God's Word. Through boldly preaching the Gospel, Paul broke the power of Diana and saw multitudes in the city receive the Lord Jesus Christ.

That's the scriptural method: preach God's Word! This is exactly what Paul advised Timothy to do as the young man pastored the growing Ephesian church that his beloved mentor had planted.

> All scripture is given by inspiration of God, and is profitable for doctrine, for reproof, for correction, for instruction in righteousness: That the man of God may be perfect, thoroughly furnished unto all good works. **I charge thee** therefore before God, and the Lord Jesus Christ, who shall judge the quick and the dead at his appearing and his kingdom; **Preach the word;** be instant in season, out of season; reprove, rebuke, exhort with all longsuffering and doctrine.
>
> 2 Timothy 3:16 – 4:2, emphasis mine

Dealing With Diana Today?

There was a demonic power reigning in Ephesus, but Paul didn't gather "intercessors" and "prayer warriors" to do battle. He told people the truth, saw them born again and set free, and discipled them to go out and do the same. God's Word is what set people free. The truth is what broke Diana of the Ephesians' power!

Several years ago, the leaders of the intercession and spiritual warfare movements went over to Ephesus (in modern-day Turkey). They believed God told them that the biggest demonic power in our day and age was Diana of the Ephesians. They thought she was the principality actually controlling the many Muslim people living in the most unreached parts of the world called "The 10/40 Window." At the amphitheater in Ephesus (ruins from Paul's time), they gathered about 20,000 "intercessors" and "prayer warriors" from all around the world. All they did was pray and do "spiritual warfare" in order to "destroy" Diana of the Ephesians.

They didn't preach the Gospel. They didn't go over there to share the truth of God's Word and win people to the Lord. Instead, they all assembled and simply held a prayer and praise service in which they supposedly "dealt with" Diana of the Ephesians. That's exactly opposite what Paul did!

Personally, I don't believe that "Diana of the Ephesians" is even a factor today. She was defeated 2,000 years ago by Paul and the fast-spreading truth of the Gospel. Nobody worships Diana today! Of course, "spiritual warfare" people would say that she's the same demonic entity behind the Islamic faith. However, that's a completely subjective argument. It's what their impressions are, but there's no way to biblically clarify and verify it. Therefore, I don't believe it's true.

Yes, there are demonic entities operating in the world today. They're there because people have empowered them through yielding to their lies. The way to change the situation isn't by dealing directly with the demons in prayer. Their power is cut off when people believe the truth. As individuals, families, and communities come out of deception, demonic powers are weakened and broken.

Who Came First?

Many Christians think that San Francisco has demonic powers of homosexuality and lesbianism hovering over the city and keeping those people in bondage. There probably is a greater concentration of those particular spirits dwelling there than in other places, but how do you deal with them?

The spiritual warfare people try to deal with it through intercessory prayer, spiritual mapping, prayer walks, binding the devil, and other similar kinds of things. That's not the scriptural New Testament model. These demonic powers are really a non-factor, other than the fact that people have yielded to and empowered them. You can't just bind those principalities and command them to depart!

Some Christians think that if you just got rid of the demonic powers, then the people would be set free to respond to the Gospel. That's completely backwards! When the people respond to the truth, the demons will lose their power and leave.

Who came to San Francisco first—the demons or the homosexuals? Some people who were homosexuals, or favored them, were elected to places of power in the government. They passed laws giving special welfare benefits, legal benefits, and other things that made San Francisco attractive to homosexuals. Therefore, homosexuals from all around the country and the world flocked to San Francisco. There weren't demonic powers already there who drew these people. The homosexuals came and brought their demons with them.

You don't get rid of the homosexual demonic powers by going into the heavenlies and doing battle directly with them. Preach the truth instead. As these people understand and believe that God loves them and made them Adam and Eve, not Adam and Steve, they'll be set free. Then they'll resist those devils with the truth, and the entire climate over San Francisco will change.

"The Soul That Sins Shall Die"

I have friends who believe that the United States won't see revival until the atrocities done in the past to the Native Americans are repented of and forgiven. They think we must do "spiritual warfare" to dislodge the demons that came to power over our country through broken covenants and innocent bloodshed centuries ago. Again, this contradicts New Testament Scripture. You might be able to quote some Old Testament verses, but these concepts don't square with God's Word this side of the Cross.

Ezekiel prophesied that every individual would answer for their own sin—and no one else's—under the New Covenant.

> *What mean ye, that ye use this proverb concerning the land of Israel, saying, The fathers have eaten sour grapes, and the children's teeth are set on edge? [i.e., "generational curse"] As I live, saith the Lord* God, **ye shall not have occasion any more to use this proverb in Israel.** *Behold, all souls are mine; as the soul of the father, so also the soul of the son is mine:* **the soul that sinneth, it shall die.**
>
> Ezekiel 18:2-4, brackets mine

God doesn't judge children for the sins of their parents today. (Ezek. 18:20.)

There were many terrible atrocities committed against the Native Americans. My wife is a Native American, but she's not carrying around bitterness and harboring hurt from what happened centuries ago. However, if I met a Native American who was upset at me because of what my great, great, great grandfather did to his people, I'd apologize. It was wrong and shouldn't have happened, but it's not what's holding this man, or anyone else, in bondage today.

This man stands before God on his own. He's not a product of what happened 300 years ago. Those things might have influenced him, but it's absolutely his choice to choose life or death. If he can understand and believe the truth that Jesus Christ dealt with all sin once and for all at the Cross, forgiveness would set him free. Deception is what keeps us in bondage, and the truth is what sets us free.

I simply refuse to empower the devil! By saying that revival can't happen until we do all of these things is giving Satan power that he doesn't really have.

Europe

Christians have actually retraced the route of the Crusades (back in the eleventh, twelfth, and thirteenth centuries) through Europe. They've done penance and apologized to descendants of people they believed their ancestors hurt centuries ago. They've done all of this believing that Europe will stay in spiritual darkness until this "reconciliation" takes place. Wrong!

What's keeping Europe in spiritual darkness? They haven't heard and believed God's Word! European television channels strictly censor my programs. They often edit my teaching so much that it takes a lot of the power out of it. One time, they bleeped out something I said about spanking your kids as if it were profanity! I can't say, "Jesus is the way, the truth, and the life." Instead, I have to state, "The Bible says that Jesus is the way, the truth, and the life." I have to present it as an opinion, not a fact. God's Word has been very much hindered in the European airways. It's this lack of the truth of God's Word that keeps Europe in Satan's grasp.

All across Europe, they've passed laws against preaching the Gospel. In France, they've made it illegal to evangelize. If you laid hands on someone and prayed for their healing, you could be put in jail for practicing medicine without a license. All of these things are against the Gospel. The reason that Europe is staying in the state it's in is because they're not open to the Good News, not because of demonic powers.

Demonic powers are a part of it. They're inspiring people to take those steps. But you can't solve the problem just by doing "spiritual warfare" and binding demons; you must get God's Word into the people!

Preaching & Teaching

Christians have spent millions of dollars traveling to some of these least evangelized nations. They go over there and "prayer walk"; that is, they just walk around "binding" spiritual powers. They are specifically told not to witness to anyone—just to pray. If the same amount of money had been spent preaching the Gospel to these unreached people, there'd be revival! This is the wrong approach and it's not working!

This meeting in Ephesus with the 20,000 people who just prayed and did "spiritual warfare" occurred before the September 11, 2001, terrorist attacks. It didn't break the demonic powers operating through Muslim extremists. It never will. This is not the scriptural method of dealing with demonic influence in people's lives.

I'm doing everything I can to get the Word out! We're teaching God's Word on television and radio in America, Europe, and around the world. We distribute thousands of tapes and CDs each year. Many of our materials (i.e., audio messages, articles, and Bible commentary) are available free online. We also support many international Christian workers who are boldly preaching the Gospel. This should be the approach of the entire Church!

CHAPTER 17

A Ploy of the Devil

"Spiritual warfare," as it's popularly presented today, is actually a ploy of the devil. Consider the fruit: Christians are encouraging Christians not to preach the Gospel but just to "pray" instead. You might wonder, *Why would Satan want believers to pray more?* Simple! The devil delights when we give ourselves to praying fruitless, religious prayers.

Who do you think "inspired" the so-called "prayers" of the scribes, Pharisees, and hypocrites that Jesus so emphatically denounced? They sounded trumpets, stood on street corners, and did all these other religious things when they "prayed." If you think the devil would never encourage people just to "pray," you're sadly mistaken. Church history abounds with example after example of the enemy luring Christians into doing all kinds of impressive-looking—but powerless—spiritual calisthenics.

As believers, our focus should be on preaching the Gospel and proclaiming the truth of God's Word to all people everywhere. However, there are groups today spending big bucks to send hundreds, even thousands, of Christians around the world on so-called "missions trips" with instructions not to preach the Gospel. "Don't witness to anyone! Your job is just to walk, pray, and do spiritual warfare." Although their hearts might be in the right place and some participants' lives are positively impacted for missions, overall—it's wrong, wrong, wrong! If they took the same amount of money and effort and invested it into preaching the Gospel, distributing tracts, and sharing the truth in those nations, they'd see infinitely greater results.

Preach & Pray

It's not a matter of either preaching or praying, they should be done together. Prayer is like water to a seed. If the seed's been planted, then it needs to be watered. But you can water and water and water barren ground, and nothing will come of it. People are born again by the incorruptible seed of God's Word. (1 Peter 1:23.) Therefore, before you water, you must plant the seed!

When Paul went forth to preach, he asked his friends to pray for him: "That utterance may be given unto me, that I may open my mouth boldly, to make known the mystery of the gospel" (Eph. 6:19).

He didn't say, "Pray that people's ears may be opened to hear. Pray that demonic powers (like Diana of the Ephesians) would leave." No! Paul asked people to pray that he'd speak with revelation, authority, and power, and that miracles would be done in Jesus' mighty name.

Prayer is an important part of the Gospel, but it can never be substituted for the preaching of God's Word. Paul's boldness to share the truth literally destroyed Diana of the Ephesians' power. Finally, Demetrius and the other silversmiths came together because they were just about out of work. People had quit buying their pagan idol images. They said:

"Not only this our craft is in danger to be set at nought; but also that the temple of the great goddess Diana should be despised, and her magnificence should be destroyed, whom all Asia and the world worshippeth" (Acts 19:27).

Until the spiritual warfare intercessors recently dug her up and gave her power she didn't previously have, Diana of the Ephesians hadn't been a factor in almost 2,000 years. Such is the power of God's Word!

God has already accomplished everything. He's already given it to us in the spiritual realm. The only war we're fighting is to receive that provision in physical manifestation.

The Truth Sets People Free

How is that war fought? Is it in the heavenlies? Do we have to climb tall buildings and rent airplanes to do battle with spiritual wickedness in high places? Must we send people to foreign countries around the world to rebuke the devil over there?

If demonic powers were really the force people claim, you wouldn't have to climb a building or rent a plane to get up close to them. You wouldn't have to send people over to foreign countries to pray either. It's not like our prayers only work within a hundred-yard radius. Even if these ideas were true, you could just bind the demons from right where you are. Prayer is that powerful!

But you don't have to do those things. Preach the Gospel instead! Tell people the truth. Broadcast His Word by radio, television, and Internet. Distribute tracts, books, and other quality literature. Train disciples and send them out. Start Bible colleges and churches everywhere. At the very least, become a ministry partner and support the work of someone who's doing these things. The New Testament emphasizes the proclaiming of God's Word!

However, popular emphasis hasn't been on preaching the Word. Instead, most spiritual warfare people are into all kinds of weirdness. I've even heard accounts of public meetings where women laid on top of men and went through the motions of giving birth. They call it "travailing" and doing "spiritual warfare." Really, it's just lewd and totally ungodly. The Lord never led anyone to do that type of thing!

Am I against true spiritual warfare? No! Am I against true intercession? No! I'm just against the weirdness being called "spiritual warfare" and "intercession" today. The Body of Christ needs to reexamine these teachings in the light of God's Word and the New Covenant.

The only reason Satan is a factor is because there are so many deceived people empowering him and promoting his doctrines. If we preached only the truth, the devil would be reduced to nothing. But since there's so much error—not only in the world but also in the Body of Christ—we'll constantly be battling lies with the truth until Jesus comes back. No one has it all figured out, so we're continually renewing our minds to the truth. There are things we're fighting, and spiritual warfare is real, but it's not because Satan has all this power; it's because he's deceived so many people. The antidote isn't intercession—binding demonic powers and enlisting millions of Christians to "pray"; it's telling people the truth and seeing them set free.

Revival

The same holds true for revival. I'm for revival. I want to see the positive effects of revival sweep through America and all around the world. We need a revival, but how do we go about receiving one?

The "intercessors" say that we must pray harder, longer, and recruit more and more people—a hundred, a thousand, a million, ten million—to pray and fast with us. They view God as the one responsible for sending revival and that He's holding it back from us for some unknown reason. Since He's "not pleased," they're repenting, doing restitution, and all of these other things to appease Him so that He'll send revival.

God has already been appeased! Jesus Christ made atonement for all sin 2,000 years ago. God's not angry anymore. Through His death, burial, and resurrection, Jesus released all the power it takes for massive worldwide revival a long time ago. We just haven't been receiving it.

We need to believe what God has already done, not beg and plead with Him for revival. You start being a vessel of God's miracles to others! You begin healing the sick and raising people from the dead! I guarantee that you'll see the effects of revival. In fact, you'll have all the revival you can handle! I'm definitely for revival. But it's going to come as people yield themselves to God, not as we twist His arm more through "intercession" and "spiritual warfare."

I know that many people will reject these truths I'm sharing because they're so contrary to the mainstream theology in the Body of Christ today. Although there are only a few of us preaching this right now, I challenge you to take another look at God's Word for yourself. Study the atonement of Jesus. Follow the example of the book of Acts. You won't find "intercession" or "spiritual warfare" being done as it's promoted today. Satan is a factor, but he's not the powerful menace he's been made out to be by people who've missed the parade.

Jesus: Our Mighty Deliverer!

Visualize the triumphant procession. See Satan defeated, stripped of all power and authority, and nailed to the cross. Allow this vision of the devil—impaled and on exhibition—to sink deep into your heart. Once you've been to the victory parade, you'll never fear him again. Satan won't be able to intimidate you the way he did in the past. You'll be set free and able to boldly minister God's freedom to others!

CHAPTER 18

Put Your Faith To Work

You don't need more faith—so quit trying to get it! If you're born again, you've already been given all the faith you'll ever need. Right now, you have more than enough faith. You're just ignorant of what you've got and how to use it!

The disciples had the same problem. Notice their response to Jesus' teaching:

> *Take heed to yourselves: If thy brother trespass against thee, rebuke him; and if he repent, forgive him. And if he trespass against thee seven times in a day, and seven times in a day turn again to thee, saying, I repent; thou shalt forgive him. And the apostles said unto the Lord, Increase our faith.*

> Luke 17:3-5

Jesus had raised people from the dead, opened blind eyes and deaf ears, healed lepers, cast out devils, and done many other miraculous things no one else had ever done. However, it was His command to continually forgive—not these other things—that provoked the disciples to say, "Lord, increase our faith!"

Faith is for everyday life! It's not only to effect miraculous healing and financial deliverance. Although these things are important, it's your daily interpersonal relationships that will place the greatest demand on your faith. You've missed it if you think faith is primarily for impossible situations, like when the doctor says you're going to die or you're facing bankruptcy. Faith certainly applies to your crises, but you need faith for the people you live and work with day in and day out all week long. How else can you turn the other cheek when someone hurts you?

It takes faith to always unconditionally love and forgive your coworkers, your spouse, your children, your parents, and your neighbors. The disciples were so overwhelmed by Jesus' command to forgive—even up to seven times in one day—that they exclaimed, "Lord, increase our faith!"

More Than Enough Faith

Jesus answered, "If ye had faith as a grain of mustard seed, ye might say unto this sycamine tree, Be thou plucked up by the root, and be thou planted in the sea; and it should obey you" (Luke 17:6).

In a sense, it appears as if Jesus didn't really answer their question. They had asked, "Increase our faith," and He answered, "If you had faith the size of a mustard seed, you could do this." What the Lord was telling them was, "Guys, you don't need more faith. You don't have a faith problem. You just aren't using the faith you've already got!"

A mustard seed is one of the smallest seeds there is. It's so tiny that when you hold one between your thumb and index finger, it's hard to tell that you even have anything there. Jesus said, "If your faith is only this much—the size of a mustard seed—you could tell this tree to be planted in the sea, and it would obey you." In other words, you don't need "big" faith, or even "more" faith. You just need to learn how to use the faith you already have.

Most Christians don't have this concept today. They believe faith works but think that theirs is deficient. That's a deception from the devil! Satan has blinded us to what we already have.

You already possess the same amount and quality of faith as Jesus did when He physically walked on the earth. It's inside every born-again believer. Satan lies to Christians to keep them from understanding this. They believe faith works, but not that they have enough of it. They think it comes and goes—sometimes strong, sometimes weak. It's like they can't get a handle on it, can't hold it, and can't control it because it's intangible. That's a totally wrong attitude about faith. You have—right now—more than enough faith. You just need to use it!

A Servant Called "Faith"

Then in verses 7-10, Jesus immediately launched into a parable to illustrate His meaning. If you understand that you already have faith and you need to use what you've got, then this parable makes sense. If you try to apply it any other way, this parable doesn't make sense. The context dictates its meaning.

> *But which of you, having a servant plowing or feeding cattle, will say unto him by and by, when he is come from the field, Go and sit down to meat? And will not rather say unto him, Make ready wherewith I may sup, and gird thyself, and serve me, till I have eaten and drunken; and afterward thou shalt eat and drink? Doth he thank that*

YOU'VE ALREADY GOT IT!

servant because he did the things that were commanded him? I trow not [Old English for "I don't think so!" or "That's not how it works!"]. So likewise ye, when ye shall have done all those things which are commanded you, say, We are unprofitable servants: we have done that which was our duty to do.

Luke 17:7-10, brackets mine

Jesus was saying, "You need to use the faith you've already got! Even if it's only as big as a mustard seed, it's enough to cast a tree into the sea. You'd put your servant to work, if you owned one, wouldn't you? You already have faith. Now put it to work!"

Servanthood and slavery were an everyday part of life in Jesus' time. If you owned one, you expected them to serve you. It didn't matter that they were tired and had just come in from working all day in the fields. If it was suppertime, you expected them to serve you your food. Their time to eat was after you were finished and satisfied. They didn't eat with you, and they definitely didn't eat before you. You were the master!

In today's touchy, feely, politically correct mindset, most people would say, "Well, you shouldn't treat a servant that way!" But in the time that Jesus spoke this parable, servants and slaves weren't pampered; they were used. You didn't just allow them to lie around and do nothing all day because you didn't want to impose on them. Neither were you kind and gentle with them. You commanded them to take care of your needs before their own. You didn't have to be mean and nasty about it, but as their master, you definitely gave them orders. If you had a slave, you put them to work!

Faith should be put to work, not pampered. Not using your faith is like allowing your slave to sit on the couch and do nothing but watch television all day. Instead of growing stronger and more efficient through use, their muscles atrophy and their abilities become dull. Then you wonder why your faith isn't producing anything. You haven't put it to work! You're not using it! Start putting your faith to work the way a master uses a slave. It's not a matter of not having the servant; it's a matter of not using what you've got!

The Gift of God

Most believers are ignorant of the faith they already have. If I started giving you some testimonies of what faith has accomplished—the dead raised, blind eyes and deaf ears opened, miraculous provisions—you'd say, "Praise God! I believe those things happen."

If we were in a service where someone died and I asked, "How many believe the Lord can raise this person from the dead?" you'd agree with me that it can be done. If I asked, "How many of you believe that if I pray, this person will come back from the dead," you'd continue agreeing with me totally. In fact, you'd probably work your way up to the front so you could see this miracle happen. But where I'd lose the majority of people is when I'd say, "All right, if you believe this, you pray for them." All of a sudden, your anticipation would turn to dread. Why? Because if you're like most people, you don't believe your faith is adequate. You don't doubt that faith works; you just don't believe you have the quantity or quality of faith you need.

I could talk most Christians into saying, "I just need more faith," and get them to pray, "O God, please give me more faith!" But that would violate everything we've seen in the Word thus far. You already have faith. You already have the same power that raised Jesus Christ from the dead living on the inside of you. You don't have a faith problem; you have a knowledge problem. You don't know what you've got, nor the laws that govern how it works!

"For by grace are ye saved through *faith; and that not of yourselves: it is the gift of God: Not of works, lest any man should boast*" (Eph. 2:8, 9, emphasis mine).

This verse can be interpreted in at least two different ways. "That" speaks of your salvation, which is a gift of God and not of yourself (your own works). However, "that" can also mean the faith you actually used to receive salvation. *That faith* is also not of yourself, but "the gift of God." Can you see it?

God's Words Carry Faith

The faith it takes to receive salvation comes by hearing God's Word.

> How then shall they call on him in whom they have not believed? and how shall they believe in him of whom they have not heard? and how shall they hear without a preacher? And how shall they preach, except they be sent? as it is written, How beautiful are the feet of them that preach the gospel of peace, and bring glad tidings of good things! But they have not all obeyed the gospel. For Esaias saith, Lord, who hath believed our report? So then faith cometh by hearing, and hearing by the word of God.
>
> Romans 10:14-17

You simply cannot believe unless you hear the Word of God. God's words carry faith!

Every word that comes out of your mouth is a container. I can say things that build you up and encourage you. I could even bring you to tears of joy through complimenting and praising you. However, I can also say things to tear you down and dishearten you. I could bring you to tears of sorrow, hurt, grief, pain, and anger. Words are powerful!

Words contain either faith or unbelief. God's words are full of faith. God Himself is faith-full, and the words He has spoken are faith-filled. They are little containers full of God's own faith. You can't believe God for salvation without first having God's Word bring you His faith. It truly takes a supernatural faith in order to be born again!

Therefore, you do have God's supernatural faith in you, and it doesn't come and go. The gifts and callings of God are without repentance. (Rom. 11:29.) We just aren't using what we have, primarily because we don't know what we have.

CHAPTER 19

Supernatural Faith

The church I grew up in used several examples to illustrate how everyone had faith. They put a chair in front of me and said, "It's faith to sit in this chair. How do you know it will hold you up?" They'd say, "It's faith to go through an intersection when the stoplight is green. You're using faith that the people on the other side will stop on red." They'd also say, "It's faith to fly in an airplane. You don't know what makes it work. You don't know the pilot. These are things you regularly do that involve faith." All of this, to a degree, is faith—but it's a human faith.

God is a faith Being, and human beings were created in His image. Therefore, every person—saved or not—has faith in them because it was a part of God and is now a part of us. However, this type of faith—to sit in a chair, drive through an intersection, and fly on an airplane—is human faith. It's based completely on what you can see, taste, hear, smell, and feel. If you saw that the chair was missing a leg or two and tottered, you wouldn't sit on it. If you heard a loud metallic squeal and smelled smoke coming from the direction of the wing, you wouldn't fly on that plane. Neither would you go through the green light if you spotted someone from the other direction barreling down toward the intersection at a high speed. Sense knowledge—what you can see, taste, hear, smell, and feel—affects human faith.

However, in order to receive salvation, you had to believe in things your natural senses couldn't perceive. You've never seen God or the devil. You've never seen heaven or hell, and you've never seen a sin. You've seen people commit sin, but what does a "sin" actually look like? You can't see sin, and you can't see when it's forgiven. Yet, you had to believe in all of these invisible, intangible things. The only way you can do this is with a supernatural, God-kind of faith.

God's Faith

God's type of faith isn't limited to some kind of physical proof. He speaks forth and acknowledges things before there's any visible manifestation.

"(As it is written, I have made thee a father of many nations,) before him whom he believed, even God, who quickeneth the dead, and calleth those things which be not as though they were" (Rom. 4:17).

God makes alive the dead and calls things that be not (physically manifest) as though they were. In this instance, God called Abram (prince) "Abraham" (father of many nations) even before he had his first child. That's God's kind of faith!

God created the heavens and the earth. He said, "Let there be light," and there was (Gen. 1:3). Then, days later, He created the sun, moon, and stars. Now I'm not sure how all of this worked, but the Word clearly records that God created light before there was even a source for it to come from. God's faith isn't limited the way human faith is!

Receiving salvation is like sitting down in a chair you can't see. Human faith can't do that. You wouldn't put yourself in a position to fall and get hurt if you couldn't see or feel something. Yet, you believed God—whom you can't physically see or feel—for forgiveness of sin—which you can't physically see or feel. How did you do that? By using God's supernatural faith!

Both salvation and the faith to receive it are gifts from God. (Eph. 2:8, 9.) God's Word contains His faith. That's why you must hear it in order to be born again.

"Being born again, not of corruptible seed, but of incorruptible, by the word of God, which liveth and abideth for ever" (1 Peter 1:23).

God's Word contains the faith it takes to believe that God became flesh, lived a perfect life, and suffered our punishment in His death. It takes God's supernatural faith to believe that Jesus was resurrected and your sins are now forgiven. You can't believe these things with mere human faith. It's God's Word that brought you this faith.

You used God's supernatural faith—not just human faith—to receive salvation. It was a gift that came when you received His Word. You didn't just put your faith *in* God—you were born again by *the* faith *of* God! As sinners, we were so destitute that we couldn't save ourselves or even just believe that our sins had been forgiven. God's good news (the Gospel) had to come to us so we could receive His supernatural faith contained in it and use it for salvation.

The Faith of Christ

You used *the* faith *of* Jesus Christ to be justified.

*Knowing that a man is not **justified** by the works of the law, but **by the faith of Jesus Christ,** even **we have believed in Jesus Christ,** that we might be **justified by the faith of Christ,** and not by the works of the law: for by the works of the law shall no flesh be justified.*

Galatians 2:16, emphasis mine

You put faith in what Jesus did, but you used *the* faith *of* Christ to be justified.

Once you're born again, you also live by *the* faith *of* the Son of God.

"I am crucified with Christ: nevertheless I live; yet not I, but Christ liveth in me: and the life which I now live in the flesh *I live by the faith of the Son of God,* who loved me, and gave himself for me" (Gal. 2:20, emphasis mine).

I'm aware that other translations say, "I live by faith in the Son of God," but my conclusion after a lot of study is that the actual accurate rendering is, "I live by the faith of the Son of God."

So you were "justified [made righteous, born again] by the faith of Christ" and now "live by the faith of the Son of God" (Gal. 2:16, 20; brackets mine). This is very important!

You were both born again and now live by the supernatural faith of God Himself. That's why Jesus said, "You don't need more faith. You just need to learn how to put what you've already got to work! The faith you have is enough to see a sycamine tree plucked up and planted into the sea. Use what you've got!" (Luke 17:6-10, my paraphrase).

Doing What Jesus Did

Since the faith we were born again by and now live by is the supernatural faith of God's own Son, it has the potential to do anything Jesus did.

"Verily, verily, I say unto you, He that believeth on me, the works that I do shall he do also; and greater works than these shall he do" (John 14:12).

How can we do the works that Jesus did? Let's not even talk about doing greater works yet. How can we work miracles, receive words of wisdom and knowledge, turn the other cheek, go the extra mile, cast out demons, and walk in unconditional love? It's because you and I have the same faith Jesus used to accomplish these things. Since it's His supernatural faith—not our human faith—it's capable of doing anything He did!

However, most Christians say, "Well, I'm only human, you know. I'm just a man." That's stinkin' thinkin'! I *was* only human, but then I became born again. There's part of me now that's wall-to-wall Holy Ghost. There's a part of me now that has the faith of the Son of God. Yes, the flesh part is still capable of failure and everything else. But the born-again part of me is powerful!

If you stayed conscious of and focused on the fact that you have the faith of the Son of God, you'd see a difference in what you're hoping, expecting, and believing for. When you truly believe that you have this potential inside, you won't put up with defeat, discouragement, and a mundane life anymore. You have and now live by the faith of Jesus Christ Himself!

The Measure of Faith

God gave every born-again believer *the* measure of faith.

"For I say, through the grace given unto me, to every man that is among you, not to think of himself more highly than he ought to think; but to think soberly, according as *God hath dealt to every man the measure of faith*" (Rom. 12:3, emphasis mine).

It's not *a* measure, but *the* measure of faith!

Most Christians think that God dishes out faith using many different measures. They believe He gives this person a ladle full and that person a tablespoon. This one gets a teaspoon and that one an eyedropper. That's totally inaccurate! God gives every believer the same measure of faith—a ladle full—because it's *the* measure of faith.

Reinhard Bonnke—the powerful German, world-healing evangelist who has preached to crowds of well over a million at a time in Africa—was being interviewed once on television. Someone in the audience asked the question, "Why do you see so many more miracles happen overseas than here in the United States? Is it because they have more faith?" My ears immediately perked up to hear his answer.

"You Americans are the only people I've ever encountered who have this concept of 'more faith.' Either a person believes or they don't. You don't have to have 'big faith.'" Then he gave some examples of people who had just heard God's Word for the first time and received. "This whole concept of 'big faith' and 'little faith' is erroneous. It's wrong!"

Faith Is a Fruit

You may be wondering, *But what about the centurion in Matthew 8? When the Lord heard what he said,* "he [Jesus] marvelled, and said to them that followed, Verily I say unto you, I have not found so great faith, no, not in Israel" (Matt. 8:10, brackets mine). Some people point to that and say, "Right there is a scriptural precedent. Jesus said he had 'great faith.'"

A couple of things are involved here. This was prior to the New Covenant and the new birth (the New Covenant didn't technically take effect until Christ's work of atonement was complete). Under the Old Covenant (before the Cross), people put their human faith in the promises of God. I'm not saying they didn't have faith, but it was different than the way a New Testament (post-Resurrection) believer has faith. It's through the new birth that you receive a born-again spirit. That's where your new nature and the faith of Christ reside. Old Testament people didn't have access to this.

Also, faith is a fruit of the Spirit.

"But the fruit of the Spirit is love, joy, peace, longsuffering, gentleness, goodness, faith" (Gal. 5:22).

Old Testament saints didn't have the indwelling presence of the Holy Spirit. He came upon them at times, but He didn't live in them the way He does now with New Testament believers. So it was a different way for them (the centurion and others like him) to believe God prior to Jesus dying for our sins, resurrecting from the dead, and people being born again.

Even after the new birth, some believers manifest great faith and others manifest very little, if any. But it's inaccurate to say that some Christians have "big" faith and others have "little" faith. Many people only use a small portion of the faith God has given them. But the truth is, every born-again believer has the measure of faith—the faith of the Son of God! (Rom. 12:3; Gal. 2:20.)

Acknowledge What You Have!

You don't have a faith problem; you have a knowledge problem! In order to see your faith work, you need to understand and acknowledge what you have.

Paul prayed, "That the communication of thy faith may become effectual by the acknowledging of every good thing which is in you in Christ Jesus" (Philem. 1:6).

Don't ask God for more, praying, "Lord, increase my faith!" Instead, believe God's Word, and begin to acknowledge that when you were born again, you were given the supernatural faith of God.

CHAPTER 20

The Law of Faith

Peter had this measure of God's supernatural faith. He healed a lame man at the entrance of the temple. (Acts 3:6-8.) People were healed as his shadow touched them. (Acts 5:15.) He even raised Dorcas from the dead. (Acts 9:39, 40.) These are the kinds of things Peter's faith produced.

Notice to whom he addressed his second letter:

"Simon Peter, a servant and an apostle of Jesus Christ, *to them that have obtained like precious faith with us* through the righteousness of God and our Saviour Jesus Christ" (2 Peter 1:1, emphasis mine).

Peter didn't earn this faith through good works but received it when he was born again "through the righteousness of God and our Saviour Jesus Christ."

With Peter, you obtained this "like precious faith" when you were born again. It's *the* measure of faith. (Rom. 12:3.) If you don't believe this, you might as well rip 2 Peter out of your Bible and throw it away! Why? Because he wrote it to those of like precious faith!

You don't have a faith problem; you already have the faith of the Son of God. However, in order to see the supernatural results Peter did, you need to learn how to exercise it!

Discovering How to Use It

I was baptized in the Holy Spirit during a miraculous encounter with the Lord on March 23, 1968. Immediately, I experienced a quickening inside and just began to understand things. Passion and a new motivation rose up from within, and I started seeing some people healed (cancer, sickness, deafness). Although I still saw only a small percentage of the large amount of folks I prayed for healed, that was a lot better than before! My faith had begun to work, and I started to realize that it was a powerful force. But I didn't yet know that I had the measure of faith—the faith of the Son of God.

So I sought the Lord and asked Him for more faith and more faith and more faith. In the process, I became frustrated. Then God revealed to me this truth I've been sharing with you. It made a huge difference in my life! Instead of begging the Lord to give me more faith, I started praising and thanking Him for what He'd already given. I began diving into God's Word—not to get faith—but to better understand what I already had and how it operated. Through studying "faith" in the Word, I started understanding the laws that govern faith and how to cooperate with them.

Faith for salvation comes by hearing the Word of God. (Rom. 10:17.) Then, after you're born again, you have God's supernatural faith in you. (Rom. 12:3; Gal. 2:16, 20.) Therefore, when you study the Bible and hear God's Word preached as a Christian, faith is already present. You're just discovering what you've been given and how to use it!

That's why you're encouraged when you read 2 Peter 1:1. You can honestly say, "I have the same precious faith that Peter had. He had the measure of faith; I have the measure of faith. Paul had the faith of the Son of God, and so do I. Anything Peter did, I can do. Anything Paul did, I can do. Anything Jesus did, I can do. Glory to God!"

Faith Follows God's Rules

Grace and peace be multiplied unto you through the knowledge of God, and of Jesus Christ our Lord, According as his divine power hath given unto us all things [faith is certainly one of these] that pertain unto life and godliness, through the knowledge of him that hath called us to glory and virtue: Whereby are given unto us exceeding great and precious promises: that by these ye might be partakers of the divine nature.

2 Peter 1:2-4, brackets mine

Before salvation, hearing God's Word brings faith to you. If you'll accept it, you can be born again using the faith that came to you through the Word. Then, once you're born again, you already have faith on the inside. It's a fruit of the Spirit. But reading and understanding the Word gives you knowledge of what you already have. The Word teaches you how faith works so that you can cooperate and receive the manifestation of your salvation benefits more completely.

You do have the supernatural faith of the Son of God, but since it's His faith, it has to follow His rules. You can't use God's faith just to do your own thing. It's not yours; it's His! In a sense, you're borrowing it. The only way this supernatural faith will produce results is if you use it in the manner God wants you to.

Technically speaking, it's not your faith. Some people say, "I'm of the Baptist faith," and others respond, "I'm of the Episcopal... Methodist," or "Presbyterian faith," as if there are different Christian "faiths." However, Ephesians 4:5 reveals that there's just "one Lord" and "one faith"—God's faith. You can't just choose to believe any old way, because if you believe wrong, it won't work. You must use that faith the way God wants you to because it's His supernatural faith, not your human faith.

God's Word speaks of "the law of faith."

"Where is boasting then? It is excluded. By what law? of works? Nay: but by the law of faith" (Rom. 3:27).

Although this isn't the main point of Romans 3, it's still a true statement. God's faith in you operates according to "the law of faith."

Constant and Universal

Faith works according to the laws God created to govern its use. The word *law,* in this sense, means "constant, without fluctuation or variation" and "universal." That means faith works for everyone, everywhere, in the same way, much like the law of gravity.

Gravity is constant—without fluctuation or variation—and universal (applying to everyone on earth). That's why we call it a "law." For instance, I'm here in Colorado using the law of gravity to sit in a chair. If, for some reason, you couldn't do the same over in China, gravity would be a "phenomenon" and not a law. In order for something to be classified as a "law," it has to apply the same way to everyone everywhere.

Most people don't look at faith as being governed by law. They think God could do anything He wants to if they just ask Him and "believe." They don't understand that there are certain restrictions the Lord has placed upon Himself. Therefore, God's faith always abides by these laws.

Again, this truth is evident in the natural realm with the law of gravity. What happens if a person jumps off the Empire State Building? Does God want to see them die? Is the Lord punishing them? No. But He won't suspend the law of gravity in order to save their life either. God doesn't want people hurt and killed by gravity, but that's exactly what will happen if they violate this law.

That's the Way It Is!

Faith is governed by law. God did that for your benefit. He doesn't want you to die of sickness, fail financially, or suffer mental and emotional problems. However, if you don't learn how faith works and begin to cooperate, these same laws (which were meant to bless you)—when violated—will kill you. That's an awesome truth!

God cannot—because He will not—violate His own laws. It's against His righteous and holy nature. When God says something, that's the way it is. He doesn't change things He's established just

175

because of our whims, needs, or ignorance. People—whom God loves with all of His heart—die not because it's His will, but because they violate His laws of faith.

CHAPTER 21

Faith Speaks

One of the laws of faith is: You will have what you say.

"A man's belly shall be satisfied with the fruit of his mouth; and with the increase of his lips shall he be filled. Death and life are in the power of the tongue: and they that love it shall eat the fruit thereof" (Prov. 18:20, 21).

Death and life are in the power of your tongue! This is a law of faith.

God created the worlds by faith through speaking them into existence. (Gen. 1.) Everything natural—physical, what we can see, taste, hear, smell, and feel—was created by words. God's faith-filled words are what framed this universe and continue to hold it together. (Heb. 1:3; 11:3.) If He were to violate His own words—the laws He created—the whole universe would self-destruct. Why? Because creation is held together by the power of God's living Word!

God's creation is governed by laws. One of the laws of God is that we have what we say. There is power in words. We speak words.

The ability to speak reflects God's image in us. This is one very important characteristic that sets the human creation apart from plants and animals—we speak words. In a sense, it's God-like because words have the ability to create.

Learn To Speak Life

Jesus confirmed this law. (Matt. 21:18-22; Mark 11:12-14, 20-24.) He spoke to a fig tree and commanded it to die. The next morning, His disciples discovered that overnight, the tree had done exactly that. In response to their amazement, Jesus declared:

> Have faith in God. For verily I say unto you, That **whosoever shall say** unto this mountain, Be thou removed, and be thou cast into the sea; and shall not doubt in his heart, **but shall believe** those things **which he saith** shall come to pass; **he shall have whatsoever he saith.**
>
> Mark 11:22, 23, emphasis mine

Faith is released by words. It's one of the laws that govern faith. Death *and* life—not just life only—are in the power of your tongue.

If you've been born again, you have the faith of the Son of God. Since most Christians don't know this, they don't use it. The few who do believe, still may not see it work properly because they don't understand and cooperate with these laws that govern faith.

If your doctor told you that you're going to die soon, your words will affect what you receive. If you knew that God had already healed you and you're trying to believe, your words will determine what you experience. You'll get life or death according to what you say. If someone asks you how you are, you release death by answering, "I'm going to die. The doctor said I've only got a week left." If you start planning your funeral and giving in to grief, you're empowering death. Even though you have the faith of the Son of God inside you, it won't be released. Instead, what Satan wants to do will be released through those words of death. Your words are that powerful!

Heart and Mouth Together

You may have heard an extreme version of this truth through the "faith" or "confession" movements. Some people have even termed this "name it and claim it" or "blab it and grab it."

This truth—you'll have what you say—has been abused in many ways. If someone said "That tickles me to death!" the self-appointed "Confession Police" would immediately jump up and condemn them. However, Romans 10:10 clarifies the issue.

"For with the heart man believeth unto righteousness; and with the mouth confession is made unto salvation."

It's only when the heart and mouth work together in faith that the confession is brought to pass. The reason why people don't drop over dead when they use a slang expression like "It tickles me to death!" is because they didn't mean it in their hearts. I'm not saying it's good to continue using such an expression, but it didn't come to pass because the words weren't what the heart truly believed.

Regardless of how this truth has been misrepresented and abused, it's still a truth. Many Christians are missing out on what

God has provided for them in the spirit because they aren't using their words properly. You must learn to speak life instead of death!

Speak to the Mountain

But just speaking your faith isn't enough; you must also speak directly to the mountain.

"Whosoever shall say unto this mountain, Be thou removed..." (Mark 11:23).

Most Christians are busy talking to God about their mountain instead of talking to their mountain about God. The mountain is your problem, or whatever you want to see changed. Speak to it!

Don't say, "O God, I'm sick. Please take this disease from me!" or "Father, please remove this debt." That's a violation of what this scripture is telling you to do. You're talking to God about your mountain. Speak to the sickness. Talk to your bills. Address your depression, or whatever else the problem may be. Tell it that God has already set you free. Then, command it to leave you alone. That's why you must understand the authority God has given you and how it works. (My teachings "The Law of Faith" and *The Believer's Authority* thoroughly address these issues.)

I stayed with a couple while ministering in Charlotte, North Carolina. They watched the video "Niki Ochenski: The Story of a Miracle." This testimony of how the revelation of grace and faith helped a teenage girl on the brink of death receive her healing deeply touched the wife. She had a friend who was suffering from the same thing (fibromyalgia and chemical sensitivities). So she immediately invited her over so I could pray with and minister to her.

Once the friend arrived, I shared God's Word and countered this woman's wrong thinking for about half an hour. When she was ready to pray, I commanded all pain to leave her body and—BOOM—it was instantly gone. She started praising God, but a few minutes later remarked, "I still have a burning across my waist in the back. Why didn't it leave with all the other pain?"

I shared with her Mark 11:23 and answered, "The Bible says you have to speak to the mountain. You told me you had pain throughout your body, so I spoke to pain. Now watch this. I'm going to speak to burning." Then I commanded burning to go in Jesus' name. Immediately, it was gone, and she was praising God!

"Burning, in the Name of Jesus..."

I taught her how to stand on the Word and what to do if a symptom returned. Then, as she was getting ready to leave twenty minutes later, she said, "That burning is back."

I told her, "Well, I've just instructed you in what to do. Now I want you to pray and rebuke this."

So she prayed, "Father, I thank You that it's Your will to heal me and that You've already healed me. By Your stripes, I was healed. I now claim my healing, I stand on it, and I thank You for it in Jesus' name." That's a pretty good prayer coming from a woman who less than an hour before had thought God sent her this sickness to glorify Himself.

However, I knew that burning hadn't left. So I asked, "How do you feel?"

She responded, "The burning is still there."

"Do you know why?"

"No."

"You talked to God about your mountain instead of talking to your mountain about God. You didn't speak to it."

"What do you mean?" she asked.

"You didn't speak to burning."

"You mean to actually call it by name and talk to it?"

"Yes, that's exactly what you're supposed to do! Talk to that burning." Many people think that's weird, but Jesus spoke to a fig tree. In fact, the Word says that He "answered" it. (Mark 11:14.) You can't answer something unless it's been talking to you first. That's why when your checkbook speaks to you and says, "God's Word doesn't work. You're going to fail. I'm in the red again!" you need to answer it with, "God's Word does work. He's El Shaddai—More Than Enough! I command you, checkbook, in the name of Jesus to come into the black and stay there!" You must speak directly to your mountain.

This time she said, "Burning, in the name of Jesus..." She stopped right there and shouted, "It's gone!" She didn't even get so far as to command it. Just by addressing it directly and using her faith in Jesus—BOOM—it left. What an awesome example of this principle in action!

Electricity

Words are important! You can't speak death, discouragement, defeat, and depression and then expect to receive blessings. It's not going to work! Why? One of the laws that govern faith states that you will have what you say. Not only must you believe God's Word in your heart and speak in agreement with it from your mouth, you must also speak directly to your problem and command it to get in line. Thank God for what He's already done, and then command your body to quit hurting, your finances to work, the devil to get off your case, etc. Take your authority and use it. These are some of the laws that govern faith.

You already have the faith of the Son of God. You just need to learn how to use it. Once you understand how it works and begin to cooperate, you'll start seeing results.

God created the natural laws that govern electricity. Even though man didn't discover them and how they operated until recently, they've been here on the earth since the very beginning. People 4,000 years ago could have used electricity, but they were ignorant of its laws. Now that we've learned the laws of electricity, we use it. In fact, we use it all the time, and it's dependable.

God didn't withhold electricity from people because they were bad. David was a very godly man, but he didn't know about it. Neither did Moses, Gideon, or Solomon. It was simply their ignorance of electricity and the laws that govern its use that prevented them from receiving its benefits. If they had known, they could have received.

People hurt themselves and die today, not because they're bad people, but because they violate the law of faith. God isn't against them. It's just that He's established laws regarding how His power flows—and they're not cooperating.

Learn what those laws are, and put them into practice for your benefit. Until you do, God's not going to change all of creation for you. He won't suspend the law of gravity to save your life and kill millions of others just because you jumped off the Empire State Building. That's not how it works. Discover the laws that govern faith and cooperate!

Release Your Faith

I've only discussed a few laws thus far (mostly related to speaking), but there are many, many more. As you study God's Word, you'll see them. You'll learn that Jesus encouraged people to act on their faith. Since "faith without works is dead," actions are another very important way to release your faith (James 2:26). There's also forgiving others (Mark 11:25, 26), and so forth.

God's Word brings you the original faith when you're born again. Then, after you're saved, it teaches you how that faith works. If you can believe that you have the same faith that raised Jesus Christ from the dead already dwelling on the inside of you, then the rest is just learning how to cooperate with the laws governing how it works.

CHAPTER 22

―――――――

Aggressive Receiving

Mark's Gospel records an awesome example of the laws of faith in operation. A woman with an issue of blood came to Jesus seeking healing. She simply touched the hem of His garment and was instantly made whole. The Lord felt virtue flow out of Him and turned around, asking, "Who touched My clothes?" (Mark 5:30).

His disciples were amazed. There was a multitude of people surrounding Him, and they were all pushing up against Him. But there was something very different about this woman's touch. She touched Him in faith—and instantly the power of God flowed!

Most people believe that, as God, Jesus knew all things. Therefore, when He inquired, "Who touched my clothes?" He was simply asking a rhetorical question. Even though Jesus was totally God in His spirit, He lived in a physical body. Although it was a sinless physical body, Luke 2:52 reveals, "And Jesus increased in wisdom and stature, and in favour with God and man."

She Said

Jesus didn't know all things in His human mind. I believe He meant just exactly what He said when He asked, "Who touched Me?"

This is a significant point. If Jesus didn't know who touched Him, then how did this healing virtue of God flow out of Him to effect this woman's cure? Think about that!

Most people think God sizes us up when we come to Him with a request. Depending on how much we've prayed, studied the Word, fasted, lived holy, or a multitude of other things, He either grants or rejects our request. But that's not what happened here. How did this woman receive her healing?

She put the laws of faith into action, and the power of God automatically flowed.

"For she *said*, If I may touch but his clothes, I shall be whole" (Mark 5:28, emphasis mine).

It's a law of God that we have what we say. (Mark 11:23.) She said and she received.

Earnest Action

It's also a law of God that "faith without works is dead" (James 2:20). This woman acted on her faith. She didn't just speak about being healed. She acted on that faith even at great personal risk.

In that day, anyone with an issue of blood was unclean, and everyone they touched became unclean also. Therefore, people with this uncleanness had to avoid crowds, because they would defile everyone they touched. She could have been stoned to death by this multitude if they knew her secret. This is probably the reason why she was hesitant to come forward with what she had done.

Notice also that she touched the hem of Jesus' garment. How do you touch the hem of a garment when there's a multitude thronging the One wearing it? The only logical explanation is that this woman was probably on her hands and knees, crawling through this mass of people.

Why is that important? It illustrates another law of faith—earnestness. You can't receive the things of God by just passively seeking them.

"And ye shall seek me, and find me, when ye shall search for me with all your heart" (Jer. 29:13).

As long as you can live without your healing, you will. But when you get aggressive, like this woman, where you are willing to risk even your own life in order to receive, you will.

Who's Crazy?

This woman had been suffering from this condition for twelve long years. (Mark 5:25.) She spent all the money she had trying all the different cures of that day but just became worse. (Mark 5:26.) No one faulted her for going the natural route. I'm sure people gave her much sympathy and pity. But if her friends knew what she intended to do—to approach Jesus in the midst of a multitude—I'm sure someone would've told her that was crazy.

It's not crazy when we let doctors experiment on us. We allow them to treat us in ways that'll kill a well person and cost us everything we have. But when we openly trust God for our healing, then we're "fanatics."

However, it takes this type of aggressive attitude to effectively receive from God.

This woman put a number of the laws of faith into operation, and the healing virtue of God flowed to her automatically.

It's Not Personal!

Remember the laws of electricity? When someone flips the light switch on the wall, the electrical power just flows. They don't have to call the electric company and ask for the power to be sent; it's already available. We just have to take the authority granted us and command the power to flow.

Likewise, when someone touches a live electrical wire, if they are grounded, the current just flows. The electric company doesn't size them up and say, "I'll teach them a lesson. I'll give them the shock of their lives!" No. There are just laws that govern how electricity flows. It's not personal.

That's the way it is with God. The Lord isn't healing one and refusing another. There are laws that govern how His power works. We can violate those laws and miss out on the blessings He's already given us, or we can learn what the laws are, cooperate with them, and experience the abundant life He's provided. It's up to us.

Ignorant of God's Laws

People could have been using electricity thousands of years ago. It wasn't the Lord that just recently made electricity available. It was man's ignorance—lack of specific knowledge—that's kept us in the dark.

My use of the word *ignorance* isn't intended as a derogatory statement. Leonardo da Vinci was a brilliant man. He invented a helicopter and many other things that were centuries ahead of his time. But he was ignorant of electricity.

In the same way, there are many wonderful Christians who are sincere and very godly people in many ways. But they are ignorant of God's laws of faith. Therefore, they aren't receiving the results they desire. They aren't bad people; they just don't know the laws that govern how God's kingdom works.

Receiving from God isn't about how He feels toward you. If that were the only issue, then we'd all be perfect in every way. It's what He wants for each and every one of us! But there are laws that must be put into effect in order to receive the things He has for us. It's our misuse of these laws that is literally killing us.

CHAPTER 23

Unbelief Counteracts Faith

Just because you understand that you already have the faith of God doesn't mean it'll automatically produce victory in your life. Your unbelief will counterbalance and short-circuit that faith until you get rid of it. Your problem isn't a lack of faith but rather too much unbelief!

Jesus and three of His disciples went up on the Mount of Transfiguration. He was glorified, and they saw Moses and Elijah speak with Him. Immediately after this, they came down from the mountain to a multitude. A man came forward to Jesus, "kneeling down to him, and saying, Lord, have mercy on my son: for he is lunatick, and sore vexed: for ofttimes he falleth into the fire, and oft into the water. And I brought him to thy disciples, and they could not cure him. Then Jesus answered and said, O faithless and perverse generation, how long shall I be with you? how long shall I suffer you? bring him hither to me" (Matt. 17:14-17).

This man brought his "lunatic" son to Jesus. Mark 9:17-22 reveals that this "dumb spirit" produced violent seizures much like what we'd call "epilepsy" today. The father had brought his boy to the disciples first, but they weren't able to cast the demon out.

Jesus was not pleased! Notice His reaction:

"O faithless and perverse generation, how long shall I be with you? how long shall I suffer you? bring him hither to me" (Matt. 17:17).

This is important because there aren't very many people operating in the supernatural power of God in the Body of Christ today. We aren't seeing very many demons cast out or people healed. As a whole, the Church seems powerless to expel devils and cure sicknesses.

Excuses, Excuses

Basically, much of the Body of Christ excuses this by saying, "Well, we're just people. We pray and ask God to do it, but if we don't see anything happen, that's just because God is sovereign and it must not be His will," or "Those things passed away with the apostles." We've come up with all these different doctrines to justify our powerlessness and ineffectiveness.

Jesus didn't respond that way. If He were like a modern-day touchy, feely, feel-good type of minister, He would've said, "Guys, I'm sorry! I shouldn't have been up on the mountain being transfigured and talking to My Father for so long. I left you alone to handle problems that are beyond your ability. After all, you're only human. Forgive me. I'm sorry. I'm here now. Bring the boy to Me." Jesus didn't do that. Instead, He became angry and thundered, "O faithless and perverse generation! This isn't the way it's supposed to be. How long am I going to be with you? How long must I be here to do these things?"

Jesus had been training His disciples. He'd already given them authority to cast out devils and heal the sick. They should have been able to handle this. So Jesus, in effect, was saying, "Guys, this isn't acceptable. You are faithless and perverse. This is not the way it's supposed to be!"

Although I say this in love, I pray that it registers and makes the impact it should: *Our Christianity today is faithless and perverse!* The Church is supposed to have the answers for the world, but we aren't using what we've got. God has already given us everything, but we aren't releasing it. We're powerless and ineffective. Most believers have simply lowered the standard by saying, "Miracles and supernatural power passed away with the first-century Church," and those who do look for miracles approach it as, "O God, we ask You to do it," instead of receiving what He's already done, taking their authority, commanding, and making it come to pass. It's twisted from what the Lord meant it to be!

Jesus' response to the disciples is the same for us today: "This is wrong! It's not the way I intended it to be." People ought to be able to come to us for healing, deliverance, and blessing (emotional and financial). But when the sick come to a typical minister today, that minister will send them to a doctor. The poor are sent to the government or some other social agency. When the mentally or emotionally disturbed ask for help, they are sent to a "shrink." This should not be! God's answers are in the Word and the Church. We shouldn't have to send people anywhere else! The Body of Christ has really failed in this area.

This is a big reason why more people aren't coming to Christ. The Church has failed to portray the Lord as the One with the answers to all the problems of life. The typical church deals only with issues of eternity and leaves all the present issues to man's ability. People just don't see the relevance of the church to everyday life. This should not be! Jesus isn't any more pleased with this today than He was in this situation with the child suffering from seizures.

Despite Prior Success

"And Jesus rebuked the devil; and he departed out of him: and the child was cured from that very hour. Then came the disciples to Jesus apart, and said, Why could not we cast him out" (Matt. 17:18, 19).

That's a valid question because Jesus had already given them power over the devil.

"And when he [Jesus] had called unto him his twelve disciples, *he gave them power against unclean spirits, to cast them out, and to heal all manner of sickness and all manner of disease*" (Matt. 10:1, brackets and emphasis mine).

Not only did they already have all the power they needed to see that demonized boy set free, they had prior success in using it!

"And they [the disciples previously] cast out many devils, and anointed with oil many that were sick and healed them" (Mark 6:13, brackets mine).

These were not people who had never flowed in God's power and the miraculous. These were followers of Jesus who apparently had a 100 percent success rate before this, which makes their question even more significant.

These were believers who had seen God's power flow through them before to heal the sick and cast out devils. They knew it was God's will and that He'd already given them the power. Yet, they exercised their faith, acted on it, and spoke to the mountain, but still didn't see the desired results. Sound familiar?

You've probably had a situation in your life when you released your faith, acted on it, spoke to the mountain, but still didn't receive your desired results. You believed God for healing, prosperity, deliverance, or whatever, but it didn't come to pass. I'm not talking about those who pray, "God, if it be Your will," and aren't surprised when nothing happens. These disciples were shocked, hurt, and surprised. They asked this question because they did believe, and they'd seen it work in the past, but not this particular time.

Why do you think certain demons don't come out? Why are specific individuals not healed? Why don't financial breakthroughs come sometimes? Why do you think people pray, really believing, but what they ask for doesn't come to pass? Although there are multiple reasons for this, the dominant answer to this question is, "It must not have been God's will." Hogwash!

"God's Will?"

God wants you to prosper in every area of your life! It's not God's will for you to be sick, to not have your needs met, to be oppressed. It's not God's will for you to be discouraged and defeated. He isn't punishing you or trying to teach you something. That's simply not true!

A large segment of the Body of Christ lumps every "unanswered" prayer into "Well, God is sovereign." God is Almighty and He can do anything He wants to, but He's already done what He wants and has given us the authority and power to bring His will to pass.

Many things happen today, not because it's God's will, but because we're reaping what we've sown. Take, for instance, the terrorist attacks that happened on September 11, 2001. Many people viewed them as "God's judgment on America." Well, America is worthy of being judged, but the Lord isn't releasing His judgment. Neither did He "sovereignly" allow it. God has set up laws that we reap what we sow. (My message "The Sovereignty of God" deals with this.)

America has been systematically trying to become a secular nation. We've kicked God out of our schools and public lives. We've been busy doing our own thing and ignoring Him. By denying God the right to move freely in our society, our defenses were down.

Satan attacks whether you're godly or not. You don't have to be doing something wrong in order to draw his attack. You could actually be doing something right and be attacked. David had people attack him when he was seeking and serving God. Although he won, he was still attacked and had to fight. It's just that there's often more damage when your defense is down.

"Because of Your Unbelief"

When we ask the question, "Why don't things work?" two main perspectives—both wrong—come forth. First, many people think,

Que sera, sera. Whatever will be, will be. God is sovereign and He controls everything. Second, a popular charismatic "faith" answer would be, "They don't have enough faith." That's presented as being the *only* reason people don't see their answer to prayer. It's too simplistic and condemns people because it puts all the responsibility on them without any grace. This drives them away from faith-oriented teaching. It is *a* reason, but not an all-encompassing one!

In ministering to another person, their faith does affect the process. You can't make them receive based on your faith alone. Jesus quickened people's faith when He ministered to them. He told them "Sin no more, lest a worse thing come unto thee" (John 5:14), implying that they had a part to play in their healing. We know that Jesus operated in faith perfectly. Yet, He couldn't do many miracles in His own hometown. This wasn't because of any problem with His faith, but the people were full of unbelief. There needs to be some degree of faith present on the part of the person receiving. However, if the healing doesn't manifest, it could also be a problem with the minister's faith and ability to receive from God.

It's just not always as simple as, "Believe and receive or doubt and do without." Sometimes you can believe and still not receive. That's what happened to the disciples here. (Matt. 17.) They asked, "Jesus, why couldn't we cast the demon out? We believed and received, but didn't get our desired results."

"And Jesus said unto them, Because of your unbelief" (Matt. 17:20).

Many people mistakenly think they can't have both unbelief and faith at the same time. They believe that faith and unbelief are mutually exclusive. That's not true.

When Jesus told them, "It's because of your unbelief," He wasn't saying, "You didn't have faith." He didn't mention that. In fact, Christ's very next statement was:

"I say unto you, If ye have faith as a grain of mustard seed, ye shall say unto this mountain, Remove hence to yonder place; and it shall remove; and nothing shall be impossible unto you" (Matt. 17:20).

It doesn't require a "great" faith or a "big" faith to do great things. You just need to minimize the unbelief working against your faith.

"Only Believe!"

That's why Jesus answered the disciples' request, "Lord, increase our faith," with, "Guys, you don't need more faith. Just use what you've already got. If your faith is the size of a mustard seed, it's enough to cause this tree to be uprooted and planted in the sea. Nothing is impossible to you" (Luke 17:5-6, my paraphrase). Notice the same terminology in Mark 11:23:

"For verily I say unto you, That whosoever shall say unto this mountain, Be thou removed, and be thou cast into the sea; *and shall not doubt in his heart*" (emphasis mine).

It's possible to be in faith and doubt in your heart at the same time!

On His way to minister to Jairus' daughter, the woman with the issue of blood touched Jesus' garment and received healing. During this delay, news came from Jairus' house: "Don't trouble the Master any longer, your daughter is dead."

"As soon as Jesus heard the word that was spoken, he saith unto the ruler of the synagogue, Be not afraid, only believe" (Mark 5:36).

Only believe! Why would Jesus tell him to only believe? Because you can believe and disbelieve at the same time!

Jesus told the father of the lunatic boy who needed deliverance, "If thou canst believe, all things are possible to him that believeth" (Mark 9:23).

Immediately, the man "cried out, and said with tears, Lord, I believe; help thou mine unbelief" (Mark 9:24).

Jesus didn't rebuke this man for saying he had both faith and unbelief. He just ministered to his son and saw him delivered. This lack of rebuke speaks volumes!

According to God's Word, you can have a true faith—that under normal circumstances would bring about the desired deliverance—but still not see it produce the right results. The problem isn't an absence of faith, but the presence of unbelief.

The Net Effect

Faith and unbelief are opposing forces. Unbelief counteracts your faith. Instead of trying to get more and more faith, you need to deal with the unbelief that's counterbalancing it. That's how you get your faith to work!

If you hitched a horse up to a thousand-pound weight and had it exert enough force, the weight would move. However, if you hooked up another horse to it on the other side and had it pull with equal power in the opposite direction, the weight wouldn't move. Even though tremendous power is being released, the net effect on the weight would be zero. That's the way it is with faith and unbelief.

Your faith is sufficient. Jesus Himself said that even a mustard seed of faith can uproot a tree or move a mighty mountain. Therefore, your faith is more than enough to see a healing, cast out a demon, or anything else. The problem is unbelief countering your faith and causing a net effect of zero.

I've seen people who obviously didn't believe it was God's will for them to be well. They fought against it when I came to pray for them. Since they didn't believe, they died. That's relatively easy to deal with. But I've also seen other people who believed it was God's will for them to be well. They were praying and trying to trust God for their healing. Some had even seen others healed or been healed themselves before. However, they still died. Now that's harder to deal with.

Confused

Many people wonder, *Why weren't they healed? I know there was faith present!* I've seen people who loved God with all their heart and were facing death with joy, yet had an expectancy and an anticipation that they'd see physical healing manifest. But still they died. Even though faith is intangible, you can tell if it's present or not when you're seeking God. When you recognize that faith is present but you see different results than what the Word of God promises, it can cause a tremendous amount of confusion.

This is why the disciples were confused when they couldn't cast the demon out of the lunatic boy. (Matt. 17:19.) They had faith, power, and authority and had successfully used it, until then. They spoke to the mountain and commanded the demon to come out. They acted in agreement with their faith, but still the results remained contrary. Why?

"Because of your unbelief" (Matt. 17:20).

Unbelief is subtle. Many people don't recognize it. They just look at a person and if they perceive faith, they think that faith will automatically work. Not necessarily! Jesus told His disciples, "It's not that you didn't have faith. It's because you had unbelief." Then, to reinforce His point, Jesus added, "If your faith is only the size of a mustard seed, it's enough to cast a mountain into the sea" (Matt. 17:20, my paraphrase). As a born-again Christian, your God-given supernatural faith is more than enough to accomplish anything you need—as long as there isn't any unbelief counteracting it!

CHAPTER 24

Wigglesworth Had Less

I went to Omaha, Nebraska, to minister not long after seeing someone raised from the dead. I knew my faith was working and things were going good. A paralyzed man in a wheelchair had come to the service. In my excitement, I reasoned, *Since my faith has developed to the point of seeing someone raised from the dead, surely it can handle a man in a wheelchair!* So I walked over, grabbed this fellow by the hand, and lifted him up out of his wheelchair. He immediately fell right over on his face!

When that happened, my faith evaporated. Everyone in the audience gasped, moaned, and groaned. I then wrestled this guy back up into his wheelchair and said the scriptural equivalent of:

"Depart in peace, be ye warmed and filled" (James 2:16).

Although I tried to encourage this man to continue believing God, I couldn't help him.

I returned to my hotel room that night totally perplexed. "Lord, what happened? I know I had faith!" It takes faith to do something like that! Have you ever yanked someone up out of their wheelchair and immediately seen them nosedive into the carpet? Most people haven't! Why? They don't believe they'd be healed. The reason I pulled him up out of the wheelchair was because I truly believed he'd walk. Even though faith was present, I didn't see the desired result. This brought me much confusion.

I sought the Lord for an answer to this dilemma for two or three years. Then, finally, I recognized my problem while reading a book about Smith Wigglesworth.

Meet Smith Wigglesworth

Wigglesworth lived in England in the early 1900s and had a powerful miracle ministry. He traveled to several countries and saw many great things happen. In this book, Wigglesworth's son-in-law recounted numerous testimonies.

At the beginning of a meeting, Wigglesworth liked to boldly announce, "The first person up here will be healed!" Someone would come forward, he'd pray for them, and they'd be healed. Wigglesworth used this as his attention-getter before delivering the message. Then, after the Word, he'd pray for the rest of the sick.

One time, an elderly woman with cancer in her stomach came to the meeting. The cancer was so large that she appeared to be nine months pregnant. She was so frail and weak, her two lady friends had to each take an arm and hold her upright in her seat. They knew what Wigglesworth was going to say, so when he made his usual announcement at the beginning of the meeting, they popped right up and brought their friend to the front for prayer.

Wigglesworth looked at her, saw this huge tumor on her belly, and told the two women holding her, "Let her go!" They answered, "We can't let her go! She doesn't have strength!" He raised his voice and said it again, "Let her go!" So they did.

"Let! Her! Go!!!"

She fell forward on that tumor and groaned in pain. The audience immediately gasped in unbelief. It was the exact same response I'd received after that man in the wheelchair fell on his face. I started feeling pity, sympathy, and embarrassment for both this man and myself. In my situation, I responded in a manner of unbelief. However, Wigglesworth stood his ground and simply said, "Pick her up."

Those two ladies picked her up. Then he said, "Let her go!" They cried, "We can't let her go!" Wigglesworth boomed, "Let her go!" When they finally did, she fell face first on that tumor again. The crowd moaned and groaned. Wigglesworth said, "Pick her up." So they picked her up once more.

Then Wigglesworth said for the third time, "Let her go!" Those two women argued, "We will not let her go!" Wigglesworth commanded, "You let her go!" Then a man in the audience stood up and yelled, "You beast! Leave that poor woman alone!" Wigglesworth shouted back, "You mind your business; I know my business." He turned to the two ladies again and barked, "Let! Her! Go!!!"

When they did, the tumor fell out of her dress onto the stage, and she walked off totally healed.

The Difference

So what was the difference? Wigglesworth and I both had "the measure of faith" (Rom. 12:3). I had enough faith to grab the man by the hand and lift him up out of the wheelchair fully expecting him to walk. However, I also had unbelief.

I was too easily swayed by what other people thought, as well as by fear, embarrassment, and pity for this guy.

"How can ye believe, which receive honour one of another, and seek not the honour that cometh from God only" (John 5:44).

When you're worried about looking good in the sight of people, it can hinder your faith. Wigglesworth didn't have more than I did; he had less—less unbelief.

Wigglesworth was often criticized as being "too hard." He would hit, punch, and even kick people at times. When asked why, he responded, "I'm just out to get the devil. I can't help it if their bodies get in the way!" He once kicked a baby with a head injury off the stage and into the front row. But that baby was healed! Wigglesworth understood the difference between godly compassion and human pity. He recognized that pity stops the power of God from operating. So he was hard, insensitive, and unfeeling toward unbelief.

Drain It to Zero!

Like Jesus' disciples in Matthew 17, I had both faith and unbelief working at the same time there in Omaha. It's not that my, or their, faith wasn't strong enough. There was just too much unbelief counteracting it.

Picture two outdoor thermometers: one measures faith, the other unbelief. Most people ignore the unbelief and concentrate on their faith. If their faith is up an inch but what they've prayed for still hasn't come to pass, they think they need to push their faith up another inch or two. So they go on an all-out effort to increase their faith saying, "O God, give me more faith. I need more faith!"

The Lord said, "It's your unbelief that's the problem. Without unbelief working against it, your faith doesn't need to be any bigger than a mustard seed to get the job done" (Matt. 17:20, my paraphrase). Instead of trying to shoot your faith through the roof, pull the plug on your unbelief. Drain it to zero, and you'll find your faith strong enough to accomplish anything you need.

Most Christians don't receive what God has already supplied because of unbelief, not lack of faith. These are two opposite situations. If someone doesn't believe, of course they won't receive. Faith is the bridge that brings God's provision from the spiritual world over into the physical world. Faith must be present, but it's not that big of a deal. It's not hard. As Christians, we have the supernatural faith of God. It's just that most believers haven't yet realized or dealt with their unbelief.

What is unbelief? It could be fear, worry, or care. If the doctor tells you you're going to die and you start trying to believe God by confessing, "Jesus, I believe that by Your stripes I've been healed," but in your mind you're still worried, that's being double-minded.

Double-minded people won't receive anything from the Lord. (James 1:7, 8.)

Mark 11:23 says, "That whosoever shall say unto this mountain, Be thou removed, and be thou cast into the sea; *and shall not doubt in his heart*" (emphasis mine).

You can't believe, be saying and doing some of the right things, and yet have a split heart. To get the results you're after, you must be single-minded and focused! (My teaching *Hardness of Heart* will answer many of your questions about this. It's one of the greatest things the Lord has ever shown me.)

"He Considered Not"

Abraham didn't allow himself to think on anything contrary to what God had told him. He was strong in faith because the promise was all he considered.

> *Who against hope believed in hope, that he [Abraham] might become the father of many nations, according to that which was spoken, So shall thy seed be. And being not weak in faith, he considered not his own body now dead, when he was about an hundred years old, neither yet the deadness of Sarah's womb.*
>
> Romans 4:18, 19, brackets mine

You can't be tempted with anything you don't think. Therefore, overcoming temptation, unbelief, and failure begins in your thoughts. If your thoughts are only on God, then all you'll be tempted with is to believe and trust Him. But if your thoughts are on things other than God, then you could be tempted with that.

Abraham didn't consider—study, ponder, deliberate, examine—his own body now dead nor the deadness of Sarah's womb. When God told him that Sarah would conceive and give birth to a child the next year, Abraham didn't dwell on his age or the fact that Sarah had long since passed the time of childbearing. The thought may have crossed his mind, but he didn't consider it.

Just because an occasional contrary thought crosses your mind doesn't mean you're in unbelief. You can't stop the devil from giving you a thought, but you don't have to keep it. As Kenneth E. Hagin often said, "You can't stop a bird from flying over your head, but you can prevent it from making a nest there." A fleeting thought doesn't mean you're in unbelief. But when you consider, entertain, study, deliberate, examine, and ponder it, you'll be tempted.

Baptized in Unbelief

Most people in Abraham's shoes today would blow it. If the Lord came to them at ninety-nine years old and said, "Your wife will have a child next year," they'd feel bound to seek a doctor for medical confirmation. "Is this possible? Have you ever heard of anyone one hundred years old having a baby? Please, examine my wife. She's already quit having her menstrual cycles. How could she possibly have a child now?" The doctors would agree and speak forth their unbelief saying, "No, it's never happened before. And it can't happen now either!" Then they'd go back to God in prayer and ask, "Lord, did You really say this?" He'd answer, "Yes, I did!" Then they'd try to believe Him after accumulating and pondering on all of these contrary thoughts. They'd wonder, *Why is it so hard to receive from God?*

The reason why Abraham was such a strong man of faith wasn't because he had more than we do. He had less—less unbelief! This man was so mentally disciplined at age ninety-nine that when told by God that he would have a child, he didn't even think about, focus on, or study his own body nor the deadness of his wife's womb. Abraham only looked at the promise of God!

Unbelief comes through your thought process.

It doesn't take a huge amount of faith to receive from God, just a pure, simple, childlike faith. However, most Christians are baptized in unbelief. We're still so plugged in to the world's negativity that it's a miracle our faith has accomplished what it has. We take in all the junk on television, radio, and movies. After subjecting ourselves to all of this bad news, God tells us He's going to do something contrary to what the rest of the world is experiencing, and we have a hard time only believing. We know God wants to bless us. We're asking for it and heading in that direction, but we're loaded down with all of this unbelief.

A Separated Life

As a young man, Lester Sumrall once visited Smith Wigglesworth. With a newspaper rolled up under his arm, he knocked on the door. After introducing himself, he asked, "May I come in and visit with you?" Wigglesworth answered, "You can come in, but that paper has to stay outside."

Now, reading the newspaper isn't a sin. I read it on occasion—once every month or two. I'll also watch a news program on television about the same. In the car, I'll listen to the two-minute news summary on the radio. But that's basically the news I get. I don't do more, because there's so much negativity and unbelief in there.

Wigglesworth probably missed a dozen or two good things in the newspaper over those thirty-five years or so. He could have used them in his messages to help make a point (like I do sometimes). But he also missed hundreds of thousands of negative thoughts and statements that could have produced unbelief in him. To Wigglesworth, it just wasn't worth the risk!

Since Wigglesworth lived such a separated life, he simply wasn't as susceptible to unbelief as I was when I tried to pull that man out of the wheelchair. Now that God has shown me this, I've started living a more separated life too. I don't watch or listen to things I used to. Because of this, some people say my faith is stronger. Actually, it's purer. It's not as diluted now. I don't have as many thoughts of unbelief as before, because I quit opening myself up to things that give me opportunity for it.

The Problem

Jesus told His disciples, "Your unbelief is the problem. If you had faith as small as a grain of mustard seed, it would be sufficient. You could have seen this boy delivered if you would have only believed" (Matt. 17:20, my paraphrase).

Taking into account the parallel passage (Mark 9:14-29), we can see some of the reasons why the disciples had unbelief in this instance. The boy had a seizure, fell down, and foamed at the mouth. I don't know if you've ever been around someone having an epileptic seizure, but I have. It'll make the hair stand up on the back of your neck!

When that happens, it'll foster unbelief, worry, and fear. It's going to look contrary to what you're praying for. And unless you've spent time specifically fighting against that type of unbelief, you'll succumb to it.

That's what happened to me when I pulled that man out of the wheelchair and didn't see the right results. I was worried about what the audience thought. I let other people's unbelief and the fear of their rejection influence me. It hindered my faith.

Faith was present, but so was unbelief. If I had stood the way Smith Wigglesworth did, then my faith would have worked the way his worked. The difference wasn't our faith, but our unbelief. I had more than Wigglesworth—more unbelief!

CHAPTER 25

Deal With Your Unbelief

Unbelief comes in three different forms: ignorance, disbelief, and natural.

Ignorance is when someone just doesn't know the truth. They might not have grown up in church, or they might have been raised in a traditional denomination. Therefore, their idea of Christianity is skewed. They think Christians are just waiting on heaven and that there's no real victory to be experienced in this life. Due to their lack of knowledge, they have unbelief.

This type of unbelief is relatively easy to deal with. Just tell them the truth! If their heart is open to the Lord, they'll receive it. Then, ignorance leaves and they're able to believe God.

Disbelief comes from being taught wrong. Someone told them, "God doesn't heal or do miracles anymore. All of that supernatural stuff passed away with the apostles." That's beyond, "Well, I've never heard of a person being healed today" (ignorance). It's, "If tongues, healing, or miracles happen today, it's of the devil." That's wrong teaching!

Disbelief is more difficult to overcome than ignorance. A person who's been taught wrong has prejudices against the truth. It's a lot harder for them to renew their mind and receive.

I had to struggle to renew my mind to the truth. I'd been taught many excuses for why God doesn't do miracles today, how tongues were of the devil, and why the supernatural things in the book of Acts don't happen now. Although it is a little harder to overcome, the antidote for this second type of unbelief is the same as the first. I had to receive the truth of God's Word above man's traditions in order to overcome this unbelief that came through wrong teaching.

Natural Unbelief

The third kind of unbelief is what I call "natural" unbelief. It's not ignorance or wrong teaching but simply natural input that's contrary to the truth. The demonized boy had a seizure and foamed at the mouth. (Mark 9:14-29, parallel to Matt. 17:14-21.) When something like that happens, your mind, emotions, eyes, and ears are all going to tell you, "The demon didn't come out. Look, it didn't work!" That's not necessarily evil, just natural.

You go through life receiving input from your eyes, ears, and feelings, and making your decisions based on that. It's not wrong, or evil; it's just natural. If you were driving me somewhere in your car, I'd want you to have some of this "natural" input. I certainly wouldn't want you driving "by faith" with your eyes closed! However, there are things you can't perceive with just your five physical senses, and there are times the Lord will ask you to take a step of faith. That's when you must be able to get beyond this kind of unbelief that comes from natural things.

If you pray for someone to be healed and they fall over dead, some natural unbelief will come at you. You prayed for them to be well, but now they're dead. What's going to happen? Unless you are really strong, you're naturally going to have fear and unbelief come up and say, "Well, it didn't work. Why? Because I can't see it!"

Most people are dominated by their physical senses. It was this kind of unbelief—natural unbelief—that hindered the disciples in Matthew 17. They believed they could cast out devils. They had done it before. The very fact that they asked, "Why could not we cast him out?" (Matt. 17:19) showed they had faith. They had ministered to the boy, believing, but when he began going into convulsions, they were moved more by what they saw than what they believed.

"This Kind"

How do you overcome this kind of unbelief? By knowing the truth and renewing your mind to it, you can get over ignorance and disbelief. But how do you get beyond what you see and feel? How do you get to where you're believing only and not letting that pain you feel in your body convince you that "No, it didn't work"? Jesus gave the answer in Matthew 17:21:

"Howbeit this kind [of unbelief] goeth not out but by prayer and fasting" (brackets mine).

Many people have misinterpreted this verse. They think Jesus was talking about "this kind of demon." So they've invented different doctrines saying that certain demons are stronger than others and can only be cast out through prayer and fasting. That's not what Jesus was talking about.

You will never encounter a demon—or even the devil himself—that won't cower and flee at the name of Jesus and faith in His name. Your fasting and prayer doesn't add anything to it. If the name of Jesus and faith in His name won't defeat the devil, neither will your prayer and fasting!

Unbelief is the consistent subject of both verses. (Matt. 17:20, 21.) "This kind" in verse 21 refers back to "unbelief" in verse 20, not to the demon in verse 19. Therefore, Jesus was saying that this type of unbelief—natural unbelief—can only come out by much prayer and fasting.

"Come Back Into That Body"

Your faith is enough. I know. I've seen three people raised from the dead—including my own son. I didn't have "big" faith. I just had simple faith.

God set me up the first time. I'd been praying for months for this man who was paralyzed from the waist down. He had been unable to move before, but I'd helped him to where he could move his legs, get around, and do things. I just went by his house every day to pray for and minister to him.

Then one evening, while I was preparing to start a service, this man's son came in and waved me down. When I walked over, he threw me—and my guitar—into his car and drove us straight to his parents' house. It didn't take but a second to get there.

(Pritchett, Colorado, only had 144 people at the time.) I just thought we were going to pray for his father, that maybe he'd had a heart attack and was in some pain.

As I walked in, the sheriff was there trying to get his oxygen mask out. The man's wife was crying and praying, "O God, please bring Everett back from the dead!" That's the first time I realized he was dead. Since I already had so much time and effort invested in this man and his healing, the first thought that came to me was, "No way!" So I walked over and said, "Everett, in the name of Jesus, come back into that body." BOOM—he just sat up healed! (Later that day, the doctor checked him out and confirmed it.)

Just a tiny bit of faith is sufficient if there isn't anything to counterbalance it. If you would've told me two days before that somebody was going to die and I'd have to raise them from the dead, my mind would have had time to start thinking. Thoughts of natural unbelief would have come at me, and it's very possible that I wouldn't have seen him raised from the dead. But the way it happened was a divine setup. God brought me over there in my ignorance. I prayed and didn't have time to disbelieve God. That's why it worked!

Prayer & Fasting

However, natural unbelief normally kicks in through your senses whenever you pray and something contrary happens. This is because you've been trained to go by your five natural senses— what you can see, taste, hear, smell, and feel. Jesus said that the only way you can overcome this kind of unbelief is through prayer and fasting. (Matt. 17:21.)

Unbelief that comes from your physical senses isn't necessarily evil; it's just natural. Living in this physical world, you must take into account what your senses are telling you.

A man once tried to fly an airplane "by faith," and I was stupid enough to go with him. It didn't take long before he realized that he didn't have the skill it took to fly. So he curled up into a fetal position on the floor and cried, "My God, we're going to die—we're going to die!" While he freaked out, I had to fly this tiny little plane. I'd never flown an airplane before. I didn't know what was going on. Besides all that, we were in a terrible storm. I actually had to fly that thing for an hour until this guy pulled himself together and landed us!

I don't recommend trying to fly an airplane by faith. You should have some aviation knowledge and be able to follow the instruments. You need to be able to respond to what you see and hear. There's nothing wrong with that.

However, there are times in your life when responding to what you can see, taste, hear, smell, and feel will not get the job done. You must be able to move beyond your natural senses into the spirit realm. How do you do that? Through prayer and fasting!

CHAPTER 26

Responsive to God

What do you do when your body hurts, you've already prayed, believed, received, and acted on your faith for healing—but you're still in pain? Under normal circumstances, you've been trained to respond to your body. Since it still hurts, which is contrary to what you prayed, your natural senses have conditioned you to conclude, "It didn't work." How do you overcome that and receive the manifestation of God's provision? By fasting!

Fasting retrains your body to respond to God's Word and your born-again spirit. When you fast, you're telling your body what to do. You're breaking the natural domination and control your body has been exerting over you. Your body isn't bad. It's just been trained wrong. You've been responding primarily to what you can see, taste, hear, smell, and feel.

That's okay most of the time, but you need to learn—experientially—that man does not live by bread alone but by every word that proceeds from the mouth of God. (Matt. 4:4.) By fasting, you say to your body, "Body, you need to understand that the spirit is more important than the physical. There are realities you can't perceive with this little peanut brain. In order to help you learn this, we're going on a fast. By not eating or drinking like we normally do, we are going to recognize that God is our Source. Instead of going by my appetite and letting food supply my needs, the Lord and His Word will give me strength!"

If you haven't trained it, your body will rebel at that, and your appetite will go wild. Many people have told me that they felt like they were going to die by noon the first day of their fast. They felt weak all over, had a headache, and so forth.

Did you know that it's a proven medical fact that fasting one day a week is good for you? It won't harm you but will purge your body of toxins. In fact, you don't physically begin to die until about forty days into a fast. Prior to that, it's mostly just your appetite talking, not physical necessity. Many of us could live off the fat of the land for quite some time!

Who Rules Whom?

When you fast, your body will try to maintain its control. It'll cause you to feel like "I'll never make it through the day" and attempt to coerce you to go against what you believe God has told you to do. Your body will exert itself, and your sense knowledge—what you can see, taste, hear, smell, and feel—will try to dominate you. That's when you'll have a choice: Either let your physical realm rule, or rule your physical realm.

By choosing to continue your fast, you're telling your body, "Get in line! You need to learn that you won't starve by noon the first day. You're being retrained so you can do the things God tells you to do and receive your needs met through His Word." Your body will rebel and answer, "No, I'll die!" That's when you say, "Okay, we'll make it a two-day fast." And your body will respond, "Two days! I'll die for sure!" You reply, "All right, three days!" Pretty soon your body will conclude, "If I'm going to survive this, I'd better shut up. Every time I complain, they add another day to the fast!" Over time, your body will yield.

After you get through the initial hunger pain, you can actually reach a place where you aren't hungry at all. It just doesn't bother you. If you go on a prolonged fast (the longest I've done was ten or eleven days) without food or liquids—other than water—you can actually get to a place where it seems like you don't ever have to eat again. You can bring your body into subjection to where God is literally ministering to you in a supernatural way.

Once that happens and you get off the fast, your body has learned something. Your body now knows that when you say, "By His stripes, I was healed," and it still feels pain, that there are realities beyond its ability to detect. You declare, "I'm healed whether or not I can see, taste, hear, smell, or feel it yet!" Your body will answer, "Okay," and submit.

But if you haven't ever fasted and disciplined your body, you'll pray, "By His stripes, I was healed," and your body will say, "You're still hurting. You aren't healed." You'll counter, "No, body, I am healed," and it'll respond, "Wait a minute here! Who are you to tell me anything? I tell you when to eat, what to eat, and how much to eat. You haven't given me an instruction in years. You're completely dominated by your senses. Don't tell me what to do!" Your body will rebel, and you'll submit to the natural unbelief that comes through your senses.

Fasting breaks the dominance of your natural realm over your spirit. Prayer does too!

Train Your Body

When you pray, you're speaking and listening to Someone you can't physically see or feel. Your natural mind and sense knowledge just goes bonkers, saying, "This is stupid! What am I doing?" But if you continue in prayer and make it a practice, you'll start seeing miracles and other things happen. There will be so much evidence that your prayer time is valid and God, whom you cannot see, is real that it will help retrain your physical senses. Your body will begin to recognize that there's more than what it can see, taste, hear, smell, and feel. Then when you want your body to act like it's well when it doesn't feel well, your body will go ahead and respond because it knows that there's more to it than what the natural senses can perceive.

But it won't work for a person who doesn't spend time in prayer and fasting. When they start trying to command their body to go against what they perceive with their natural senses, it'll rebel because they've never disciplined it.

Your body isn't evil; it's just natural and has to be trained. However, no one else can do this for you. You must train yourself and exercise your senses. (Heb. 5:14.)

You may not realize it, but you had to train yourself to submit to your physical senses. As a soldier in Vietnam, many nights I had bunker guard. Both my hearing and my smell became much more acute in that life and death situation. We usually smelled the

Enemy before we could see them. You can actually train yourself in these things!

Sixth Sense

Just as your natural senses can be trained in the physical realm, they can also be educated in spiritual things. They don't have to remain carnal. They can be trained to discern spiritual truth. This is what fasting and prayer does!

I believe the Lord originally created mankind with six senses. That sixth sense was faith. Adam and Eve used faith just as much as they used their other five senses. When mankind fell, our sense of faith began to atrophy to the point that today many people are total strangers to it. But this ability to walk by faith does exist within us all. It just has to be nurtured and trained.

"But strong meat belongeth to them that are of full age, even those who by reason of use have their senses exercised to discern both good and evil" (Heb. 5:14).

Our senses must be exercised in order to operate in faith. That's what fasting and prayer do. They don't make God respond to you better. Fasting and prayer make you respond to Him better.

Stick With It!

When you spend so much time in His presence, His Word becomes like a sixth sense. You might not see, taste, hear, smell, or feel what God said, but you have faith based on His Word. Your natural mind will just accept that and say, "It's not discernible by these other senses, but that's faith. I recognize it and that's the way it is." You can train yourself that way!

That's what Smith Wigglesworth did. He spent so much time in prayer, fasting, and the Word that he hardened himself toward unbelief and what other people thought. He was sensitive to God and hard toward other things. When he prayed for someone and didn't see the manifestation right away, he just kept at it until he did.

Since the Lord has shown me these things, I stick with it now until I see the manifestation. If I pray and don't see a physical manifestation, I just make it happen. I know in my heart that God has already done His part. I understand that He's already released His power. Therefore, I'm not just asking and pleading with Him to do something; I'm aggressively receiving what's already been done, and I'm standing against Satan who's hindering the manifestation. I'm taking my authority, speaking to the mountain, and commanding things to happen!

When ministering to other people, there are things you can do that will quicken their faith. Sometimes I discern unbelief while praying for someone. It may not be evil or disbelief, but maybe this person is just dominated by natural things. If they're having a hard time receiving healing from God, I'll just push over into a gift of the Spirit. Then, using a word of wisdom or a word of knowledge, I'll talk to them about something emotional—perhaps about how they've been hurt. Maybe depression, grief, or tragedy had struck. So I'll use this gift of the Spirit to speak to them on something totally unrelated to their physical healing. Then they start receiving, saying in their heart, *There's no way he could have known this. God is speaking to me through this man.* All at once, they open up and faith starts flowing. Once their faith is quickened, their heart says, *Yes, this is God. Father, I receive.*

Then I'll come back and speak to that physical healing that didn't manifest before. All of a sudden, they'll be healed. I've at least doubled or tripled the amount of people I've seen healed by doing this. That's what I mean by "making" it happen.

Positioned To Receive

God has already done everything to heal everyone. It's not a matter of asking the Lord to heal, but rather our receiving the healing He's already given. That's the basic principle, but there are laws that govern how it works. You have to speak. So I talk to the specific parts of people's bodies and command them to respond. I take authority over the devil. Sometimes I do things to quicken the other person's faith. I don't do all of these things to manipulate God but to help people move into a position to receive.

Since understanding and applying these powerful truths, I'm seeing much better results than ever before—and you will too!

Conclusion

God has already done His part. His transmitter works perfectly twenty-four hours a day. He's constantly giving us everything we need.

Our receiver is the problem, not God's transmitter. We must learn to understand the spiritual realm and cooperate in faith to bring His provision into physical manifestation.

We must stop giving the devil extra power and glory. He's been completely stripped and defeated. Remember the parade!

We already have the supernatural faith of God. Therefore, our problem isn't lack of faith, but unbelief. Our simple, childlike, mustard seed of faith is more than enough to see anything done if there's no unbelief to counteract it.

If we truly believe God's Word and are acting in faith upon it but still aren't seeing the right results—nine times out of ten it's natural unbelief. Through prayer and fasting, we can break the domination of our physical senses and begin to exercise our natural realm to respond to the Lord and His Word.

This foundational revelation has totally transformed my life! I trust that this same revolution has now also begun in you. Therefore, I pray "that the God of our Lord Jesus Christ, the Father of glory, may give unto you the spirit of wisdom and revelation in the knowledge of him: The eyes of your understanding being enlightened; that ye may know what is the hope of his calling, and what the riches of the glory of his inheritance in the saints, and what is the exceeding greatness of his power to us-ward who believe" (Eph. 1:17-19). Amen.

Receiving Jesus as Your Savior

Choosing to receive Jesus Christ as your Lord and Savior is the most important decision you'll ever make!

God's Word promises, "That if thou shalt confess with thy mouth the Lord Jesus, and shalt believe in thine heart that God hath raised him from the dead, thou shalt be saved. For with the heart man believeth unto righteousness; and with the mouth confession is made unto salvation" (Romans 10:9, 10). "For whosoever shall call upon the name of the Lord shall be saved" (Romans 10:13).

By His grace, God has already done everything to provide salvation. Your part is simply to believe and receive.

Pray out loud: *"Jesus, I confess that You are my Lord and Savior. I believe in my heart that God raised You from the dead. By faith in Your Word, I receive salvation now. Thank You for saving me!"*

The very moment you commit your life to Jesus Christ, the truth of His Word instantly comes to pass in your spirit. Now that you're born again, there's a brand-new you!

Receiving the Holy Spirit

As His child, your loving heavenly Father wants to give you the supernatural power you need to live this new life.

"For every one that asketh receiveth; and he that seeketh findeth; and to him that knocketh it shall be opened...how much more shall your heavenly Father give the Holy Spirit to them that ask him?" (Luke 11:10-13).

All you have to do is ask, believe, and receive!

Pray: *"Father, I recognize my need for Your power to live this new life. Please fill me with Your Holy Spirit. By faith, I receive it right now! Thank You for baptizing me! Holy Spirit, You are welcome in my life!"*

Congratulations—now you're filled with God's supernatural power!

Some syllables from a language you don't recognize will rise up from your heart to your mouth. (1 Cor. 14:14.) As you speak them out loud by faith, you're releasing God's power from within and building yourself up in the spirit. (1 Cor. 14:4.) You can do this whenever and wherever you like!

It doesn't really matter whether you felt anything or not when you prayed to receive the Lord and His Spirit. If you believed in your heart that you received, then God's Word promises you did. "Therefore I say unto you, What things soever ye desire, when ye pray, believe that ye receive them, and ye shall have them" (Mark 11:24). God always honors His Word—believe it!

Please contact me and let me know that you've prayed to receive Jesus as your Savior or be filled with the Holy Spirit. I would like to rejoice with you and help you understand more fully what has taken place in your life. I'll send you a free gift that will help you understand and grow in your new relationship with the Lord. *"Welcome to your new life!"*

About the Author

Andrew's life was forever changed the moment he encountered the supernatural love of God on March 23, 1968. The author of more than thirty books, Andrew has made it his mission for more than five decades to change the way the world sees God.

Andrew's vision is to go as far and deep with the Gospel as possible. His message goes *far* through the *Gospel Truth* television and radio program, which is available to nearly half the world's population. The message goes *deep* through discipleship at Charis Bible College, founded in 1994, which currently has more than seventy campuses and over 6,000 students around the globe. These students will carry on the same mission of changing the way the world sees God. This is Andrew's legacy.

To contact Andrew Wommack please write, e-mail, or call:

Andrew Wommack Ministries, Inc.
P.O. Box 3333 • Colorado Springs, CO 80934-3333
E-mail: info@awmi.net
Helpline Phone (orders and prayer): 719-635-1111
Hours: 4:00 AM to 9:30 PM MST

Andrew Wommack Ministries of Europe
P.O. Box 4392 • WS1 9AR Walsall • England
E-mail: enquiries@awme.net
U.K. Helpline Phone (orders and prayer):
011-44-192-247-3300
Hours: 5:30 AM to 4:00 PM GMT

Or visit him on the Web at: **www.awmi.net**

Other Teachings by Andrew Wommack

Spirit, Soul & Body

Understanding the relationship of your spirit, soul, and body is foundational to your Christian life. You will never truly know how much God loves you or believe what His Word says about you until you do. In this series, learn how they're related and how that knowledge will release the life of your spirit into your body and soul. It may even explain why many things are not working the way you had hoped.

Item Code: 1027-C   4-CD album

Item Code: 318   Paperback

The True Nature of God

Are you confused about the nature of God? Is He the God of judgment found in the Old Testament or the God of mercy and grace found in the New Testament? Andrew's revelation on this subject will set you free and give you a confidence in your relationship with God like never before. This is truly nearly-too-good-to-be-true news.

Item Code: 1002-C   3-CD album

Item Code: 308   Paperback

Living in the Balance of Grace and Faith

This book explains one of the biggest controversies in the Church today. Is it grace or faith that releases the power of God? Does God save people in His sovereignty, or does your faith move Him? You may be surprised by the answers as Andrew reveals what the Bible has to say concerning these important questions and more. This will help you receive from God in a greater way and will change the way you relate to Him.

Item Code: 301b   Paperback

The Believer's Authority

Like it or not, every one of us is in a spiritual war. You can't be discharged from service, and ignorance of the battlefield only aids the enemy. In war, God is always for us, and the devil is against us; whichever one we cooperate with will win. And there's only one way the enemy can get your cooperation—and that's through deception! In this teaching, Andrew exposes this war and the enemy for what he is.

Item Code: 1045-C   6-CD album

Effects of Praise

Every Christian wants a stronger walk with the Lord. But how do you get there? Many don't know the true power of praise. It's essential. Listen as Andrew teaches biblical truths that will not only spark understanding but will help promote spiritual growth so you will experience victory.

Item Code: 1004-C   3-CD album

God Wants You Well

Health is something everyone wants. Billions of dollars are spent each year trying to retain or restore health. So why does religion tell us that God uses sickness to teach us something? It even tries to make us believe that sickness is a blessing. That's just not true. God wants you well.

Item Code: 1036-C   4-CD album

Charis Bible College

Combining the rich teaching of God's Word with practical ministry experience.

You have a destiny!
Find it at Charis.

Over 70 campuses across the U.S. and around the world

Convenient distance-learning options

Start down the path to your destiny.

Visit **www.CharisBibleCollege.org** to see all our program options, or call 719-635-6029.

Harrison House

Connect with us on

f Facebook @ HarrisonHousePublishers

and 🄾 Instagram @ HarrisonHousePublishing

so you can stay up to date with news

about our books and our authors.

Visit us at **www.harrisonhouse.com**

for a complete product listing as well as

monthly specials for wholesale distribution.